D1624749

# PRAISE FOR
# BALD BEARDED BOSS

"Elliott's story is very inspiring and drew me in immediately. I believe his experiences as a child and teenager prepared him for his success today. If he didn't blow through $90,000 early, he would have learned that hard lesson later when he made millions. But in all it shows Elliott's character and his giving spirit and that's why he is so blessed today."

**—JOSHUA MUNDY,** *Co-Founder of Pivot Technology*

"Elliott is more than a dear friend. He is a beacon of light. He is a walking testimony of what can happen when one lives boldly enough to realize your potential, authentically enough to stay true to yourself and humble enough to love and learn from others. Whether you want to be the best entrepreneur, parent, spouse, friend or human you can be…this book will give you the inspiration and courage you need to do it."

**—MICHAEL BRODY-WAITE,** *Founder of the Mask-Free Movement, Author, TEDx Speaker, and Inc. 500 Founder*

"Elliott's unique story is an inspiration to entrepreneurs and business leaders who are looking for something more than just financial success. This book is a guide to finding a personal purpose and meaning in your work beyond the numbers. A truly inspiring read that will change your life."

**—JJ ROSEN,** *Founder of Atiba | Half Geek Half Human*

"I've heard Elliott tell his story many times, in different ways and at different forums. The first time it was short and just contained the basic facts: he found something he could do better and built a multimillion-dollar business around it and he discovered who he was and built a loving family life around that too. Each time I'd hear him tell his story, I'd learn there was more to it and thus more to this person who I've come to know and appreciate as a fellow entrepreneur, neighbor, and friend. This book filled me in even more about how he used his life experiences to build a successful business and a happy family."

**—BOB BERNSTEIN,** *Founder of Bongo Java*

"Through his involvement in the Nashville LGBT Chamber and the broader business community, I was aware and proud of Elliott's work and success in both. That appreciation was taken to a whole new level after reading about his journey in his own words in this book. He shares intimate moments of his life and how they shaped him into the leader he is today, and how that work is accomplished and balanced with the many parts of his identity. It is wonderful to see an LGBT leader share their success and story to help show that we all want to live our true lives and be our authentic selves and that we should be judged by our actions and work and how we make an impact.

The book speaks to Elliott's commitment to diversity and inclusion in all forms, and in business, D&I works when it is embraced at the top. This book and his understanding and commitment are a model for others to follow on the path to full equity at the office."

**—JOE WOOLEY,** *CEO, Nashville LGBT Chamber of Commerce*

"I met Elliott through being an advisor to him for his business. He is one of the best young entrepreneurs I have had the pleasure to work with. His humility, commitment, and integrity are refreshing and are clear driving forces behind his tremendous success. Getting to know Elliott is getting to know someone who knows who he is, trusts his vision, and is never satisfied with the status quo. Informed by his own life experiences, he's a true leader and embraces the challenge of running a business with his own unique and honest style!"

**—GEORGE LAZENBY,** *Co-founder and CEO of OrderInsite, LLC, a leading provider of cloud-based supply chain and inventory management software for the pharmacy industry. Former CEO of Emdeon, the nation's largest health information network, which Mr. Lazenby led through a successful IPO and in 2011 sold to Blackstone for $3 billion, and former COO of Medifax EDI, one of the nation's leading revenue cycle management companies which was acquired in 2004 by WebMD.*

"This book shows Elliott's amazing climb to success through trials, hardships, and life. The story of his climb to the top is one that spotlights one's ability to overcome any circumstance as long as one possesses drive and ambition and creates a vision. His focus on his end goal, partnered with successfully navigating life experiences, provides motivation for any dreamer looking to accomplish something great. Bald Bearded Boss is a great story that everyone will be able to see themselves in."

**—ROBERT SHERRILL,** *CEO, Author, Speaker, and Returned Citizen (granted a pardon by President Donald J. Trump while in his last days in office)*

BALD

BEARDED

BOSS

# ELLIOTT NOBLE-HOLT

# BALD BEARDED BOSS

## MANIFESTING WHO YOU'RE MEANT TO BE

*Advantage*®

Published by Advantage, Charleston, South Carolina.
Member of Advantage Media Group.

ADVANTAGE is a registered trademark, and the Advantage colophon is a trademark of Advantage Media Group, Inc.

Printed in the United States of America.

10 9 8 7 6 5 4 3 2 1

ISBN: 978-1-64225-220-0
LCCN: 2021914651

Cover design by Megan Elger.
Layout design by Mary Hamilton.

This publication is designed to provide accurate and authoritative information in regard to the subject matter covered. It is sold with the understanding that the publisher is not engaged in rendering legal, accounting, or other professional services. If legal advice or other expert assistance is required, the services of a competent professional person should be sought.

Advantage Media Group is proud to be a part of the Tree Neutral® program. Tree Neutral offsets the number of trees consumed in the production and printing of this book by taking proactive steps such as planting trees in direct proportion to the number of trees used to print books. To learn more about Tree Neutral, please visit **www.treeneutral.com**.

Tree Neutral

Advantage Media Group is a publisher of business, self-improvement, and professional development books and online learning. We help entrepreneurs, business leaders, and professionals share their Stories, Passion, and Knowledge to help others Learn & Grow. Do you have a manuscript or book idea that you would like us to consider for publishing? Please visit **advantagefamily.com**.

*This book is dedicated to my parents who instilled an excellent work ethic in me, my husband who keeps me grounded and centered, my daughter who has motivated me to be the best "me" I can be, and to my future self—I can't wait to meet you!*

# CONTENTS

# FOREWORD

The Universe has my back and I trust in its direction.

This thread of belief is no exception to my deeply valued friendship with Elliott Noble-Holt, my Bald Bearded Boss. Who I was meant to be or what my life aspirations were had little to no meaning when I sat across from Elliott over ten years ago for my first interview postgraduate school. I was sitting in front of a man who imagined his thoughts and believed in his own core values, and his inspiration was boldly recognized. I knew quickly his energy was a magnetic force—one of a kind.

Elliott took a chance on me and he became my first official boss. Organically, we quickly formed a dynamic friendship. I looked up to him and he valued my personal and professional growth. I'm proud to be his first director of operations—his right-hand man. My thoughts and who I was meant to be finally started to have real meaning because of him and our friendship.

Thank you, Universe.

The *Bald Bearded Boss* is an open and honest truth of his real-life journey that has teachable moments for all of us. It is an introspective deep dive into who we are as humans. "Live so you don't have to explain" is one of the lifelong lessons Elliott shares with us based on the evolution of his relationship with his mother and father. Through his most challenging moments of fear and loss, the guiding principles of forgiveness and reconciliation have powered how he leads his family and business today. A lesson you will learn is to trust in God and the Universe instead of being a whiner or naysayer with the mentality of "why me?"

Elliott strips away the smoke and mirrors and guides us on how to nurture relationships both personally and professionally and what it means to cultivate and maintain mutual trust and respect. He relives his experiences to impart the idea that any relationship, good or bad, helps us manifest ourselves into who we're meant to be. He motivates and inspires us to take charge of our lives, celebrate our differences, and control our own narrative. We are responsible for putting in the work, and he challenges us to be accountable and liable to ourselves. Whether you're a parent, spouse, gay, straight, entrepreneur, or a "baseballing ballerina" the takeaways are raw and real. Elliott helped me realize my visions and taught me that thoughts do become things. Luckily for me, I've had a front-row seat and now it's being shared with you. It's no secret that my friend, the Bald Bearded Boss, has the formula for all of us to achieve our own version of success.

Forever Grateful,
**Blake McConnell**

# PREFACE

*Bald Bearded Boss* is about the twin passages I made from childhood through adolescence and into adulthood. The first passage centered on my private life—the challenges I faced and the triumphs I experienced. That journey began with a happy childhood. Then, when I was an adolescent, my father left the family. It was a traumatic experience that hit me hard. I devoted my early adulthood to seeking ways to overcome it. Eventually, I was able to see the light, move forward, and create a family of my own.

The second journey was about the birth, growth, and success of my business. MediCopy, a medical information company, started with a copy machine on my kitchen table when I was not quite twenty. With perseverance and guidance from God and the Universe, I was able to build it into an award-winning enterprise valued at over seventy million dollars.

These dual journeys of my life took parallel courses and were intertwined. Personal struggles overlapped with business challenges.

Personal triumphs came with the success of the business. In the end, I learned that my life and business goals aligned.

I decided to tell my story for two reasons. I wanted to record the phases of my life and how I dealt with them. Writing a book seemed a great way to take stock of my ups and downs and make sense of them.

Perhaps more importantly, I wrote *Bald Bearded Boss* in the hope that others will read it and be inspired to push through adversarial situations and grow. I wrote it for the young African American person who is faced with hardships and wonders if they will ever achieve their goals. I wrote it for the gay or lesbian who dreams of being an entrepreneur or building a family but sees too many hurdles. Finally, I wrote it for everyone—regardless of race, background, or sexual orientation—who has a vision but is unsure how to make it a reality. I wrote to give all of them hope and show them that there is a positive path forward.

I wanted not only to share how I forged that path but to illustrate how they can do it too. I encourage every reader of *Bald Bearded Boss* to make a vision board and use it to inspire their future. At the close of each chapter, I included instructions on putting the pieces of a vision board together. By the time you complete the book, you should have everything you need to make your board. When you do, I hope you will see that with work and faith, you can make the journey of your life worthwhile. You can live your visions and achieve your dreams.

# CHAPTER ONE

# I'M GOING TO BE THE BOSS

**A**t six thirty in the morning, the sky had turned from dark-blue to gray, giving just enough light for me to make my way up the hill to the low-rise brick apartment building where I lived with my dad. The yard was soggy and scattered with patches of white, remnants of a midwinter blizzard that had covered Nashville in snow. I have always had a superstrong memory, but they say when it comes to key life events, your recall is always sharper. No wonder every single thing that happened on January 12, 1996, is etched in my mind—right down to the lyrics of the Reba McEntire song I would listen to over and over that night. It would turn out to be one of the most extraordinary days of my life.

The days that led up to that morning signaled no warning of what was coming. The snow had led my high school to extend Christmas vacation. I spent the break at the home of Vafa and Safa, two of my closest friends. We watched reruns of *The People's Court*, listened to the Cranberries, indulged in their mom's incredible cooking, and enjoyed the unexpected snow. Then we hit repeat—more television shows and heaping plates of great food. It was a special time, made even more memorable by their huge luxurious family home, decorated in the style of their Persian heritage.

School was starting back that morning—the beginning of my last semester of senior year at Glencliff High. I was looking forward to returning to my routine: a full load of classes highlighted by business management, typing, accounting, and economics; my job helping out Miss Terry in the principal's office; and of course, lunch—the Mexi Melt, Nacho Supreme, and Chicken Burrito I picked up daily at Taco Bell. I avoided the school cafeteria, preferring to eat with Miss Terry or some of my teachers.

As I reached our front door, my thoughts turned to my dad. Ever since I could remember, Tommy Holt was just about everything to me: inspiration, protector, provider, friend, confidante. A workaholic trying to make ends meet, he always held down two or three jobs. There he was rushing off to a day job in a printing company. Then over to his small side business. And I was scampering to keep up, helping as best I could. One of his gigs was a paper route, throwing the *Tennessean*, the morning newspaper. We would wake in the dark of the night and drive his dusty red Toyota Corolla to the newspaper's office to pick up papers. After stuffing the papers in plastic, we wound our way through the Nashville streets, tossing them. By the time we got home, my mom would have already left for work. Dad would get changed for his next job, and I would get ready for school.

My strongest flashback of Dad centered on the business he and my grandfather John ran. They had each put in $250, bought a

Davidson 500 printing press, and converted our basement and garage into a printing company. They had turned the downstairs laundry room into a darkroom, where they made negatives. As a five-year-old, I regularly made my way down to the basement after dinner and watched the two of them at their craft. The scene—sights, sounds, and aromas and all—is fresh in my head: the clang of the presses running, the smells of the ink and of the chemical they used to clean the eeriness of the darkroom.

On Dad's evenings off, too, he and I were inseparable. We would sit on the den floor and watch our favorite television programs—*The Carol Burnett Show*, *Alice*, *Sanford and Son*, and others. There was something about sharing those sitcoms that often sent us rolling over in laughter and tightened our father/son connection. I would even sit on the basement steps every night, sometimes even falling asleep, waiting for him to go to bed.

Then, without much warning, our father/son relationship took a sour turn. When I was about eleven, Dad started sneaking around with another woman. He tried to keep it a secret. But how could he? My mom and I would do stakeouts, driving past his mistress's house, trying to catch him. I honestly did not know what we expected to do or say if we saw him. This went on for about a year. Eventually, Dad's new relationship came out in the open, leading to a cascade of difficult events: a messy divorce; a scene in which my mom blurted out that my father did not want me; a split family, with my mom and dad getting joint custody of me; and a split family business. (My brother, Matt, and sister, Christie, lived with their other parents.)

Yet, five years later, Dad and I were living together, in that two-bedroom at Gazebo Apartments. I was just entering high school. Our bond had loosened, but it was not broken. In some ways it seemed our roles had reversed. I became more of a caretaker, constantly reminding him to brush his teeth and change his clothes. He was not making much money, so I tried to compensate with leftover popcorn and hot dogs from my job at the concession counter at a local performance auditorium. I had, for a while, also become principal caregiver to my grandmother. Following a stroke, she moved in with us. Just a few months earlier, Dad had moved her to a nursing home.

Four steps down, a turn of the key, and I was in the apartment. A rerun of *The Benny Hill Show* blared from the television. The British comic was doing one of his slapstick routines, accompanied by canned laughter. The lights were on, and Dad was dressed and half sitting up, apparently sleeping. I breezed past and into my room.

"Hey," I yelled. "Time to get up. You're going to be late again."

No answer.

"Daddy?"

I rushed over and tried to get Dad to sit up. I felt his face and then his chest. Both had gone hard. His beeper, somewhere in his pocket, kept going off, telling him he was late for the paper route. While I tried frantically to get him to wake up, every possible horror flashed in my head. I called 911, my mom, and his girlfriend. In what seemed like minutes, the apartment was filled with medics, police, relatives, and friends. I watched as a paramedic put paddles on my dad to try to revive him. The paramedic kept staring at me and doing everything he could because I was not moving.

The next thing I knew they had placed him on a stretcher, covered his face and whole body, and carried him out the back way up the muddy hill to the ambulance.

And then I remember letting go a long piercing scream.

* * *

When people are faced with grief, setbacks, or other hurdles life poses, they turn to different mechanisms to help manage. Many lean on the support of friends, family, and loved ones. Others indulge in the comforts of food, drink, or assorted earthly pleasures. And there are those who seek solace in spirituality, go into a dark space, or drown themselves with work.

*MY WAY OF COPING WAS TO START A BUSINESS.*

My way of coping was to start a business. Or, more precisely, to revive a side company my dad had owned. Odd as it seems, even as a teenager, running my own business felt like my calling. Courses I had taken in school had provided me with some business skills. An opportunity was knocking, and I was ready to answer. Even though I was still in high school, I had all the elements in place to follow through on it.

Or so I thought.

For sure, I had the kind of space in my life start-up entrepreneurs need. By nature, I avoid the difficult emotional situations that stop a lot of people. I move quickly forward. That's exactly how I dealt with this phase of my life. After the morning of Dad's passing, I left his place for good. Except for a trip to gather my things, I would never return. I left my sister to deal with Dad's belongings. Within a week, I had moved to my own apartment. My mom lived a good distance from my high school, too far for me to live with her and commute back and forth to classes. Besides, she was somewhere between staving off depression and trying to put the pieces of her life together. And so, there I was, at all of seventeen, out there on my own. For the first time in my life, I was waking up in an empty apartment. And when I came home, there was no one to join in watching TV, sharing meals, or just hanging out. A business would help me fill that blank canvas.

I also had inspiration. Entrepreneurial spirit runs through my family's blood, and I had inherited it. My three grandfathers and uncles were all small-business owners. My paternal granddad owned a gas station. My maternal granddad—and later his sons, my uncles—owned a company that sold and repaired appliances. My other granddad—John (whom my mother's mother had married after her divorce)—jointly owned a small printing company with my father. They all passed on to me the spirit and value of business ownership.

Even as a six-year-old, I would play boss, going through the motions of how I thought a business owner should act. I would sit at my father's messy desk and clean it, putting everything in order. I would clean the printing press, pick up paper off the floor, and sweep up. In that play boss world, my imagination sometimes ran wild. I pictured how I would boss people around or act as the man in charge. I even practiced answering the phone in a professional voice.

> EVEN AS A SIX-YEAR-OLD, I WOULD PLAY BOSS, GOING THROUGH THE MOTIONS OF HOW I THOUGHT A BUSINESS OWNER SHOULD ACT.

And perhaps above all, I had a business vision. One big lesson I came to understand is that being an entrepreneur should be about having a mission. I can remember watching the printing press and realizing that it created something and the product it created was delivered to other people. It didn't just stop at getting paid for a job and that's the end of it. It was something bigger. My dad and grandfather were in the business of getting information to people who needed it. They did this one print job called "Bible Class," a very small booklet, that my grandfather John still does. We used to have to print it, cut it, fold it, collate it, staple it, rubber band it, bind it up—and then these older ladies would send them to Africa to share the Word. I know it sounds crazy, but thinking about all that made me feel I was also part of that mission. I was born to spread the Word to people who need it. A printing business seemed to fit right into that.

Thankfully, Dad had left enough of a business infrastructure that I did not have to start from scratch. He and a colleague had launched a printing business in a tiny three-hundred-square-foot office space. After Dad was gone, his partner abandoned the whole thing. The office, a couple of printers, a paper cutter, and a shrink wrapper were all that was left. It seemed like that was all that we needed.

In any case, I had some capital too! My father had left me $40,000 from his insurance. I sued for an additional $50,000. My dad was ordered by the court to pay me $100,000 in the divorce decree. But in his insurance policy, he had designated that $40,000 should go to me and $50,000 to his mom. She died before she could claim it and willed it to my dad's girlfriend. I sued the estate for that $50,000, and eventually won. I received a total of $90,000. For a seventeen-year-old who had gotten used to leftover popcorn, it felt like a million dollars. That would cover my living costs and leave some money for start-up expenses for me and my brother, Matt.

I did not know much about printing, but Matt had picked up some know-how about it from my dad and granddad. The printing would be his job. I would be the sales manager. (Even though I did not know much about sales, either.) We had business cards made up and bought some beepers. MediPrint was launched!

Being the owner of my own business gave me pride and bragging rights—two things that were hugely important for a high school senior. My friends had after-school gigs at McDonald's and other fast-food places. "I have a business," I would say. "It was left to me by my dad. Here's my card."

But, of course, the business did not keep grief from gnawing at me. It seemed that nothing could. In my last semester of high school, I went from an honor roll student to barely squeaking through. I looked for the camaraderie of friends, and they came through, covering me like a blanket.

I ran through my inheritance about like any teenager would. Stupidly. My apartment was $470 a month to rent. My car note was $260. I wasn't smart enough at the time to know to pay the car note off or take some money and get a townhome, or condo, or do something else smart with it. The first day I got the money, I took four of my friends to Just For Feet. We all bought new outfits and new shoes. It was just silly. To be sure, I also helped people. I had a couple of friends whose parents were closing on a house. And so, they borrowed some. Or another friend, who needed money for a down payment on a car. So, I gave them loans. In time, they paid me back. But before I knew it, I had blown the money, all $90,000.

When it came to the business, I thought Matt and I had all the pieces in place to make it work. It turned out that we lacked some pretty basic things. The biggest was knowledge: we did not have enough training in printing to sustain the business. And my heart was not in sales. I did not know the customers or how to build a customer base. Apart from that, in his own state of grief, my brother was not wholeheartedly engaged in it. To make start-ups work, I would later learn, timing is important. And the timing for that business was just not right. After a couple of years, we closed MediPrint.

Yet, I was not defeated. The lessons of that venture stayed with me. I would eventually use them in building a company that would employ over two hundred people, earn $25 million annually, and make the Inc. 5000 list eight times in recognition of its status as one of America's fastest-growing companies.

The period when I was finishing high school and juggling life on my own was frantic. Even though I could not really articulate it at the time, I knew there were some voids I needed to fill. For one, I had to develop some work skills. After graduating from high school, I enrolled in college with a plan to study business management and started classes. After ten days I realized higher education was not for me.

Instead, I focused on my job at the Tennessee Orthopedic Alliance in the medical records office, where my mom worked. I had worked there off and on since I was fifteen.

When it was clear that I would not go to college and the failed printing business was behind me, I focused more on that job. The pay was only $4.25 an hour, but I was learning a trade. This was the era before medical records were kept electronically, so charts for the various patients had to be pulled manually and passed on to the doctors, insurance companies, or whoever else needed them. Hunting down and organizing charts and records was something I became pretty good at.

I also needed to find some balance with my newly configured family. Family has always been important to me. A year after my father passed, my grandmother died too. I had been her caregiver for a couple of years, bathing and feeding her, so her passing on the heels of my dad's was a huge blow. I turned to friends and their families. And I began seriously dating. I nonetheless felt a void.

And, just like that, someone moved in to help fill it: my mother. During my childhood, Marilyn Holt and I had not been close. She had been as much a workaholic as my dad, leaving at dawn for work and coming home in the dark. During my adolescent years, I could not recall spending much time with her. During my dad's affair, however, we had grown closer. The divorce had thrown things off base, but then, with my dad gone, she reached out. We spent time together. When I needed financial support, she responded generously. Most importantly, she was curious about what was going on in my life and began to share what was going on in hers. And she taught me important life lessons.

More than anything, I needed to come to terms with my father. I had to go through the stages of grief—from denial to, finally, acceptance. That process had started on that fateful night in mid-January 1996 when Dad died. I ended the day back at the home of the friends where I had spent the holidays, found my way into Vafa's room, and started to listen to music. As happens when I could not find the right words to express my feelings, I turned to music and lyrics. Although I was never a big fan of country, in this case it was Reba McEntire who, with her song "The Greatest Man I Never Knew," captured my feelings just right:

> *The greatest man I never knew came home late every night,*
> *He never had too much to say. Too much was on his mind.*
> *I never really knew him, oh and now it seems so sad.*
> *Everything he gave to us took all he had.*
> *Then the days turned into years, and the mem'ries to black and white.*
> *He grew cold like an old winter wind blowing across my life.*

Eventually I was able to understand and accept my dad. I would come to realize that I had to forgive him for the affair and for breaking up the family in order for me to grow. My relationship with my mom also continued to become stronger. And I was perfecting my skills at work.

Now I felt ready to move forward.

# CREATING YOUR OWN VISION BOARD

## EXERCISE ONE:
### Remembering Your Dream Job

Were you inspired by the flashback to my adolescent dream of becoming a boss? You undoubtedly had a comparable experience. As children, we constantly asked one another what we wanted to be when we grew up. "A fireman," said one of my friends. "President of the United States," called out another. Have you obtained your childhood dream job or opted for something else?

I recommend that you begin gathering the pieces you need to recapture the profession you fantasized about. Recalling what you wanted to be as a youngster will probably not put you on a career path. No doubt you have changed your mind at least once since then. But it may be a way to get you back in the spirit of dreaming big.

For starters you need poster board and glue. Then find a picture of yourself at age thirteen or younger. Next, comb through some magazines, and find a picture of someone in the job you imagined, whether it's an airline pilot, a banker, or a business owner. Then find scenes of someone in that profession at work.

As we progress through the book, we'll add other concepts to inspire you in the creation of your vision board. By the time you complete the book, we'll be ready to put the pieces together on a board.

For now, keep the parts related to your early career aspirations in a place you'll remember.

# CHAPTER TWO

# A BASEBALLING BALLERINA

For a moment—a childhood-fantasy-comes-true moment—I was on my way to becoming a dancing star. It happened at Pam's Dance Studio, where kids in Nashville learned ballet and other dance routines. My mom had enrolled me in the tap class, apparently in an attempt to nurture my dance passion. Miss Pam, lithe and chirpy, held court, demonstrating how to do the kick ball change, a primary tap dance step. And there I was, all of six years old, standing amid a roomful of girls, soaking it all in. Miss Pam walked through the steps, and I drank in every detail. I practiced in place and pretty soon had it down pat. That night I put on a show for my parents in the kitchen, demonstrating my new skill. For most of the kids, Pam's was at the very least a fun Saturday afternoon or possibly even the start of a career in the performing arts. For me, it was a chance to nurture my inner Michael Jackson. Visions of prancing across a giant stage flashed in my head.

Then, just like that, my brush with dance fame was over. All my fantasizing aside, the experience turned out to be a horror. My shoes—hand-me-downs bought from the *Thrifty Nickel*, a classified ads newspaper that sold secondhand clothing and musical instruments—were too tight and pinched my toes. But that was a minor annoyance compared to my real dread: that someone would see me leaving the class, walking from the bright pink facade and onto the street. They might know about a secret I was harboring and torture me with teasing. In that moment, I was torn. I loved everything about dancing. At the same time, I was sensitive to the possibility of being teased. In the end, my dread about what my classmates and others would say won out.

When I look back, much of my anxiety was probably rooted in the fears of a kid trying to work out some issues—sexuality, body image, what people thought of me. But at the time, my discomfort felt very real. I couldn't wait to get out of that dance class.

I know these kinds of awkward situations are not unique to me. Nearly everyone has had episodes in childhood or adolescence that leave them feeling self-conscious, ashamed, or embarrassed. Maybe it was when they summoned the courage to send a text message to a crush and got rebuffed. Or when they threw a ball and it landed right in the hands of a player on the opposing team. Or it might be something they like doing but feel uncomfortable that someone forced them into it. Often, the kid involved is thrown into an emotional whirlwind, thinking life could not get any worse. They withdraw from their friends. Or they are traumatized to the point of having anxieties.

What adds to the emotional confusion is that the circumstances around these events are rarely black and white. Sure, my shame of being seen entering or departing the dance school was real, but there were things about the dance world that appealed to me. I loved the pink satin jackets that Miss Pam and the other kids wore. And I relished the opportunity to learn new dance moves. As a kid, I got into dancing about the house. One night might find me in my bedroom, stepping to Olivia Newton John's "Let's Get Physical" in my Superman underwear and cowboy boots. Another night, I would be moving to Michael Jackson's "Beat It," sporting my sheriff's hat, thinking I was something. I would get caught up in the rhythm of songs and hitting the beat with my steps. From a distance, my mom noticed my budding dance passion and wanted to encourage it. But as a six-year-old, tap dance class just wasn't the right fit.

Fortunately, my parents pulled me out of the class early. I had not mentioned my fear about others' views if they found out I was in the study. I guess I didn't have to. Before I knew it, Little League baseball had replaced dance on my after-school schedule. And just like that, I was a member of Angel's Team. Never mind that I was not really into sports or particularly good at them. The whole Little League scene—the games, sportsmanship with other boys, and all—felt like the right track for me. I took pride in my uniform, my cleats, my hat, and all the rest of the gear. Angel's was a decent team, but that did not matter to me. What impressed me was that it was a winning team. I had a competitive winning-at-all-costs spirit, and every team victory brought me a thrill. My favorite Little League memory is of the day I got the team ball. Everyone cheered, and my parents beamed with pride. To this day, I still have that game ball.

# TEACHABLE MOMENTS

Those early adventures with dance and T-ball gave me a couple of insights that have stayed with me throughout my life. Ultimately the dance school helped me understand that I did not have to suffer things I did not like or made me tense or embarrassed. From that point on, whenever someone or something confronted me with uncomfortable scenes, I knew I had the option of either meeting them head-on or distancing myself and moving on. If I am in, I am 100 percent in. I do it on my terms. If I am not comfortable, I leave the situation behind and move on. I have made this a practice of mine.

Since Miss Pam's, this practice of deciding which road to take has helped me push past negativity. It has been the North Star that guided me away from toxic friendships, unfortunate relationships, bad business deals, and tragic workplace dramas. Many people grapple with which way to go when they come to this kind of crossroads. They wonder if it's worth it to put up with bullies or challenge them in hopes that things will change. I learned not to do that.

**I GET STRENGTH FROM LETTING THE LIGHT OF GOD GUIDE ME.**

I get strength from letting the light of God guide me. I feel like there's a portal between Him and me, and I listen to Him and have faith. And with that faith, I have confidence that what's supposed to happen will happen, good or bad. I leave fate in His—and the Universe's—hands.

One example of my decisiveness in pushing back against awkward experiences happened when I was in junior high school. I did not perform well in physical education, and I dreaded attending the class. And again, just as with dance, I feared that I would screw something up and that would lead to locker-room teasing or speculation about my sexual orientation. So I went to the teacher, Coach Singleton. "I do not want to be in your class," I told him bluntly. "What's the problem?" he asked. "I don't know," I said. "I just don't want to do this." I proposed that I work in the principal's office instead of coming to PE. He agreed on the condition that I give him a two-page report daily on my work in the office. We had a deal!

Would I have gained something from PE? Undoubtedly. Were there other ways to alleviate the stress of PE? Probably. But by trading in the PE class for office work, I was able to replace an activity that stressed me with one that fulfilled me.

As I grew older, I gained more resolve in letting go of situations—and people—that did not seem right. I learned to say no to anything that does not bring good energy, value, or satisfaction in my life. After high school, I enrolled in college mostly because it was what most people I knew did. But my realization that it was not right for me came quickly, so I walked away without hesitation. When I started dating, I would sense when it was not the right person and end it. In my business, I have parted ways with employees who were underperforming and with clients who did not share our core values. It's always good to explore ways to make situations work, but it's best to cut it off and move on if something is not right.

Of course, there have been many challenging situations that I could not avoid. I faced them head-on even when they were emotionally demanding. In most cases, after working through them, I have taken away valuable lessons. One of the earliest such experiences was going through my parents' divorce as a twelve-year-old. That caused me almost unbearable emotional pain. But it also made me appreciate and value love and loved ones. Another challenging event was my father's sudden death. As I processed that tragedy, I became aware of the importance of time. Losing someone so unexpectedly also taught me that I could take nothing or no one for granted. The lawsuit I waged—and eventually won—for my father's inheritance was also stressful. Whenever I had to go to the courtroom, I would get almost physically sick, red-faced, and a stomach in knots. From probate to appeals and finally to the Supreme Court (https://caselaw.findlaw.com/tn-supreme-court/1342055.html), the course of the lawsuit took me to a lot of hearings. Yet, there I was, sitting in the highest court in Tennessee, trying to figure out if my dead father did the right thing by leaving money to me so I could survive. I was facing stress head-on. Through it all, I learned the value of being proactive, actual, and factual.

*I HAVE MADE A PRACTICE OF FUNNELING MY ENERGY INTO PURSUITS THAT ADD SOMETHING TO MY LIFE.*

At the same time, I realized that it was not enough to walk away from things that I don't like or make me uncomfortable. I have made a practice of funneling my energy into pursuits that add something to my life. During my school years, I threw myself into math and business courses and often took away top honors. Later, starting and growing my business would become my obsession.

## EMBRACING A NEW CULTURE

In the same vein, I have also built my own circle of trusted friends and family. Many of them are African Americans. I have embraced many aspects of their culture and made it a central part of my life.

This shift toward African American culture probably originated in the times we celebrated holidays in my childhood. During these occasions, I had the chance to view my family up close and see what they were about. On Christmas, we would always drive first to the family gathering in the countryside around Lewisburg, Tennessee. This was my white family, my mother's relatives. The mood was vanilla-flavored—as if they were being forced to celebrate Christmas. They had to get in and get out. Open the gifts. Let's go. And it always seemed like they were hiding things. There was something that wasn't being said. Looking back, it's still a mystery to me why they avoided open discussion.

From there, we would return to Nashville to visit with the family of John, my African American grandfather. (My grandmother had married him after she and her first husband divorced.) From the instant we stepped in the door, the whole family welcomed me warmly. The whole evening went like that. The food was seasoned. The banter was blunt too. There was no holding back. They all wanted to be there. They cut up. They joked and joked about each other. And nobody took offense to it because it was the truth. I was attracted to that. I value that. It felt like they were so much more alive and loving and real than my mom's family. Ever since then, open and honest communication has been among my core values.

Those events prompted me to raise questions: What are families supposed to be about? What kind of family do I fit into? What were my family's values? And that made me realize that in some ways, my white family was mired in prejudice, bigotry, and hypocrisy. Still, it wasn't until a few years later that I really began distancing myself from them. It came to a head during the period of my parent's divorce and my father's death. Those events left me feeling lonely and isolated. But after the funeral and a brief period of grieving, everybody seemed ready to move on. I realized I was on my own.

With time, I would build a circle of friends—and eventually, my own family. It seemed natural and logical for me to turn to African Americans as the foundation. Having John as a grandfather gave me a look into a culture that I may have never had the opportunity to see without him. He opened a door to Black culture.

Bit by bit, friend by friend, my bonds with African Americans tightened. Of course, much of our interaction as kids was mostly about hanging out, playing. But I learned something important from each of them. Lil Mack and OJ were brothers I met when we were adolescents and their family moved into the apartment above ours. Lil Mack was always the sensible friend I could talk to, much like a loving brother. He was such a great listener, and I always knew I could call on him if I were ever in need. OJ was still pulling girls and surrounded by friends. I felt comfortable around him and his friends since he accepted me for who I was. Keisha, whom I met in school, always made me laugh and laughed at all my jokes.

The most important of these early friendships was with Nikki, whom I also met when we were both kids. She lived in the neighborhood of my childhood home, so we'd see one another a lot. Even in those early days, Nikki was smart, educated, polite, fun-loving, and funny. She was competitive too. She pushed me and gave me just the nudge I needed to get through elementary school. We both wanted to be at the top of the class. Thanks to her nudging, I was in the Top 3 Club, made honor roll from kindergarten until fifth grade, and was twice in the homecoming court. I remember her mom talking to us as kids, encouraging our friendship and healthy competition. I gained a lot of respect for Nikki. Our friendship and mutual respect have followed us into adulthood.

To an outsider, particularly in a southern city in that era, it may have seemed odd for a skinny, blond-haired, blue-eyed white kid to have a close circle of African American friends. But it was perfectly natural to me. I found a festive spirit and affirmation in those relationships. They inspired me throughout adolescence and continue to inspire me in adulthood.

This camaraderie with them, in turn, became my entree into Black culture. I preferred the music of African American artists like Michael Jackson and Bobby Brown. I was more comfortable with my Black churches than the white churches of my upbringing. When I finally forged a family of my own, it was no surprise that my husband would be African American and my daughter biracial. Later, my daughter would say my child-raising reminded her more of an African American mother than a white father. That sounded about right to me.

*  *  *

While my approach to life, friendships, family, and faith might not be for everyone, the test of whether it is right is in the evidence. It has worked for me. It has brought me business success. It has also allowed me to have a great deal of personal happiness. For sure, I have been through challenges. But I have learned to take difficult experiences in the most favorable light. I feel that God and the Universe have put me through them to appreciate them and offer them as instruction to others.

Looking back, dance school would become a moral tale for me. One of the illuminating points I learned from that experience is that you can't do everything. I left the dancer in me behind at Miss Pam's. I still get a kick out of watching others dance, particularly the backup acts in live concerts. Besides a few moves in the shower or around the house, however, I just never got back into it.

But I have held tight to my love of music. I have graduated from my seventh-grade craze when I would take my boom box on the bus and listen to Salt-N-Pepa's "Expression." These days my tastes range wide—from Janet Jackson to Mariah Carey, Kendrick Lamar, and beyond. They all give me the surge of joy that dance class once offered.

# CREATING YOUR OWN VISION BOARD

## EXERCISE TWO:
### Your First Kudos

For me, playing on the Little League team was one of the first times I got recognition from my peers. Boy was that a big thrill!

Can you recall a similar time during childhood or adolescence when someone other than your mom recognized a talent you had or an achievement you accomplished? As long as the occasion was a meaningful moment, it doesn't have to be a big award. It could have been something like getting a pat on the back from a teacher or coach.

Your assignment is to gather materials to help bring you back to that moment.

Dig through family albums to find a picture of yourself around the time the recognition occurred. Find other pictures to help recreate the scene, whether it was a sports playing field, a classroom, a church, or somewhere else. Keep all these photos in a special place. Once you're finished with the book, you can pull them out and start building your board.

# CHAPTER THREE

# TO GAY OR NOT TO GAY

I waited until Mom was sitting down. We hugged, caught up on small talk, and then settled onto the sofa in my apartment in Nashville. The moment had come for me to share a deep secret I had worked for years to keep from her. It was my eighteenth birthday, and I had my home and my independence. The time was right for me to rip the Band-Aid off. I was ready to come out to her. Once I opened my mouth, the story flowed—about my attraction to men, my first intimate encounter, my first boyfriend. As I talked, I saw the gamut of emotions—from surprise to fear—flash across her face. And then I stopped and looked her in the eyes. She was the closest person in the world to me. I cared about what she thought. I was breathless to hear her reaction.

Up until that episode, my journey of gayness had gone pretty smoothly. Sure, there had been a few speed bumps but no major dramas. I had known about my attraction to the same sex since childhood. When I was six, I acted on the impulses with a neighbor, a kid around my age. Much later, the summer I was fifteen, a schoolmate and I also fooled around.

That experience morphed into a period of self-discovery. In my late teens and early twenties, I spent time trying to figure out the stuff all gays want to know: what kinds of guys attracted me, how did I fit into the culture, and could I have children, marriage, and all the other things everybody else had? Of course, I had fun along the way. Together with my best friend Courtney—who was out and more experienced—I embarked on adventures on the gay scene. We might spend one Saturday night meeting up at a small Black gay club tucked away in North Nashville. We'd hang out with friends, drink a few cocktails, and listen to music. The next week we might catch a drag show at another club. I made friends with a few drag queens and liked to see them perform.

After my dad passed and I got my place, I jumped into the adult dating scene. I started seeing someone when I was nineteen. That relationship lasted for a while and was followed by another "long-term" partnership. In many ways, I began to feel on top of the world, finally able to let my gay self out.

I lost contact with my straight friends in that period, including Vafa and Safa, OJ, and Lil Mack. We had no fallout or hard feelings, but I deliberately distanced myself from them. For one, I wanted to avoid difficult conversations about my sexual orientation. In a way, I created barriers to protect myself. Since we circulated in close circles, I did not want them to have to be in a position to defend their friendship with me against others who might be skeptical about homosexuality or outright homophobic.

Every one of my relationships had plusses and minuses. Some of them caused real growing pains. Messing around with a childhood friend intrigued me, but it also left me feeling awkward and guilty. And when he and his family moved away abruptly, I experienced my first heartache. Over time, that unexpected separation made it more comfortable in later life for me to move on from relationships that were not quite right. And then, when my fifteenth summer ended, my close friend and I started going to different schools, and so went our separate ways. Even though our liaison seemed casual at the time, the parting plunged me into depression. One morning I woke up, took a handful of my grandmother's painkillers, and nodded off, wishing I'd never wake up. Thankfully, the medics got to me in time. When my family questioned me about what happened, I blamed it on the shock of my parents' separation.

With time, I gained clarity about what I valued in partners. I'd be lying if I said good looks were not significant. And, for sure, whoever I was with had to be financially independent. Finally, the more awareness I had about my weight and weight issues, the more important it was to be with someone comfortable with my body and physical presence.

I also got a good sense of what I could not tolerate in relationships—my deal-breakers. After viewing the pain of my father's infidelity with my mom from a front-row seat, I could not accept a partner who lied or cheated. As I became more focused on building my business, my partner had to understand and be comfortable with that.

# CONTROLLING THE NARRATIVE

While my comfort with my sexual orientation evolved positively, the control of my life's narrative was more challenging, particularly of my gay life. It was vital for me to keep my gayness private. I wanted to determine when and with whom to share the announcement about that part of my life. Until the time was right, I took drastic measures to keep my sexual orientation secret from everyone outside my small circle of gay friends. In the LGBTQ community, the need to be in charge of your own coming out and to control the story of your gayness is widely felt.

There are lots of reasons. For me, fear was one of the biggest. As a kid, I had constant anxiety that someone would find out about me being gay. I used all kinds of excuses and tactics to cover it up. Sometimes I went out to ride my bike with some of my friends. The truth was that I would probably instead have been inside playing Barbie with some little girlfriend. Or maybe I just wanted to ride around with kids from the neighborhood without having them think of me as *the gay kid*. When I was six, I had a couple of friends who lived nearby. One was a neighbor. The other was a straight friend, approximately seven years old. I had a quiet crush on him, but nothing ever came of it.

Whenever antigay sentiments surfaced in church services, Bible study, or conversations among friends, I felt my fears were reinforced. I went with my close straight Persian friends Safa and Vafa to a retreat for Bahaism, their family's faith. At one point, Safa asked, "Why are homosexuals not accepted in the Baha'i faith?" I turned red all over. Embarrassed, ashamed, and guilty as charged. I felt called out without being called out.

Even more important than my fears was my burning desire to be recognized as more than just another gay person. As proud as I am of the gay part of me, I consider it just a part— and in many ways only a small

**EVEN MORE IMPORTANT THAN MY FEARS WAS MY BURNING DESIRE TO BE RECOGNIZED AS MORE THAN JUST ANOTHER GAY PERSON.**

amount—of who I am. I don't like to be judged for being gay or being categorized as a "typical gay" or "typical white guy" or even a "typical businessman." There is nothing ordinary about me. I feel that I am among the best at most anything I undertake. In life achievements, I am part of the 1 percent. I take pride in that status and want others to appreciate that.

My thoughts about this have been shaped, in part, by observing how society often labels LGBTQ people and puts them in boxes. Many gays and lesbians buy into that. The LGBTQ chamber of commerce in Nashville is a good example. It's a worthy organization, one that is helpful to many business owners. But there is also an attitude of being in a gay bubble, limiting their options and aspirations. Some members might seek to compete for Best Gay Business Owner. In contrast, I think every business owner should be the best business owner period.

I felt the need to control my story because I was still working out who I was throughout much of my adolescence. This struggle for identity is pretty standard, but in my case, it was compounded by my depression after my parents' separation and my father's death. I would go to church with my parents and hear people quote the Bible to emphasize that marriage was supposed to be between a man and a woman, that gays would go to hell, and so on. I heard these things so often I wondered whether they were real. I battled with big questions: Was I born this way or had messing around as a kid turned me this way? In the end, I knew I had to push back against any idiot who said things like, "You're not born gay" or "This can be reversed" and all this stuff. Eventually, I was able to say, "Hold on, you can't do that to me. That's not the truth." You're not going to say that about me; it was vital for me to take control of those types of narratives. But it took some time for me to get there. It made more sense to share my gay life record when I had more security and clarity.

The importance of controlling your narrative extends beyond LGBTQ people to all kinds of groups that society tries to put in a box. In particular, African Americans and other minorities, as well as women, feel it. In some ways, the demand among minorities to tell their own stories responds to the general societal attempts to label them—or anyone who is "the other"—and put them on the side. I relate to this. In response, minorities and others outside the mainstream feel it essential to reject how they are characterized and say instead, "This is who I am; this is what I am about. I am me and not what you think I should be." I relate to that.

## SHARING MY SECRET

When the time came for me to share my secret gay story, I realized that the only one I felt the need to share it with was my mother. I did not think that it was essential to come out to colleagues, friends, or other relatives. I wished that I had come out to my father. I wanted him to know all of me. But by the time I was ready to open up about that part of my life, he was long gone. I learned from his old girlfriend that he had become aware of it before he died and that made me happy.

Finally, right there on the sofa in my apartment, I had shared the whole truth of my life with the one person I cared for most in the world. After hearing me through, my mom let her tears flow. And I let go of mine. When she slowly recovered from the shock of learning something important, new, and unexpected, she acknowledged that she was disappointed; this was not the path she would have wanted for me. With time, she expressed her unconditional love and support for me, for who I was. I talked to my mother every single day after that. And she was always supportive of my sexual orientation. She gave me her ear, and I was happy to have someone I could tell everything about my life, including my gay life.

Even though I feel that being gay is only a part of who I am, I must honor that part of my life. One way I have done that is by seeking out a life partner. Eventually, I found a man I was compatible with. After a year of dating, Donte and I married and have proceeded to build a life together, one based on mutual respect, companionship, and love. We decided we both wanted to be fathers and located a surrogate mother. At this book's writing, we began to look forward to two sons coming into our world. Most of our life together is at home, work, or vacation. But we occasionally join other friends, mostly to celebrate birthdays or other milestones. And we sometimes drop into drag shows. I have several drag queens as friends, and I like to support them.

At my business, I have worked at creating an inclusive community. By 2021 MediCopy had more than two hundred employees and a diverse workforce, with 77 percent being women and 40 percent people of color. Sixty percent of my management team are African American or LGBTQ. I have worked to assure that all my employees feel valued, no matter what their background is or who they are.

While I do not cast myself as a role model or mentor to others in the LGBTQ community, I am happy to offer guidance at my business or elsewhere. One big reason I was put through the things I experienced is to be able

ONE BIG REASON I WAS PUT THROUGH THE THINGS I EXPERIENCED IS TO BE ABLE TO SHARE MY OWN STORY WITH OTHERS— TO ILLUSTRATE THAT THERE IS A POSITIVE WAY FORWARD FOR EVERYONE.

to share my own story with others—to illustrate that there is a positive way forward for everyone. When friends, family, or team members at work approach me with questions about coming out, workplace equality issues, or navigating relationships, I share my story. I tell them that as simple as it sounds, their most effective foil against bigotry or hardship is to go about every day in the most honest, open way possible. And I try to encourage them to follow my simple but tried-and-true rule: live your best life and good things will come.

# CREATING YOUR OWN VISION BOARD

## EXERCISE THREE:
### Celebrating What Makes You Different

Everybody has something that distinguishes them from the mainstream. For me, one of those things was being gay. Coming to terms with my sexual orientation was a journey. And controlling the narrative about who I am was one of the most challenging parts of that experience.

Including in your vision board images that center on an aspect of what makes you different can be a powerful and rewarding experience. For many people of color, one of the key characteristics that sets them apart is often race, particularly if their workplace or school is predominately white. Women often find themselves in the workplace surrounded by men. Gender might be what distinguishes them. For others, it might be sexual orientation or something else.

To prepare for this section of your vision board, I suggest first pinpointing something that sets you apart. Then identify others you admire who share that characteristic. For some people of color, it may be some other very well-known person of color. For LGBTQ people, it may be other gays or lesbians whom you admire or respect. Keep these images with other materials you've gathered for your vision board. This will serve as a visual reminder that even if you're different, you are not alone. Appreciating the strength in numbers often gives you resilience.

# CHAPTER FOUR

# FAMILY BEFORE EVERYTHING

t was a chilly December afternoon when I called my daughter to the meeting. Within minutes, we were both in tears. Throughout my years of fatherhood, I had known this moment was coming. And I had dreaded it every day. From the time Isa was a kicking, screaming newborn, through birthday celebrations and weekly father/daughter breakfast dates, I rehearsed in my mind what I would say, and I always cringed with anxiety. By then, she had become a poised young lady of thirteen. It was time. So, there we were, sitting across from one another in a conference room at my office. I knew I could no longer avoid telling my daughter the truth: that she had been adopted.

I had planned to share the news when Isa turned eighteen. At that stage, I felt she would be able to absorb it with minimal shock. In the meantime, I placed my focus on nurturing her. Every day I found ways to demonstrate how much I loved, respected, and supported her. I knew Isa absorbed and accepted all this. I was also aware that when many adoptees learn of their adoption, the event sometimes becomes traumatic. This was precisely what happened in one family I knew. When the parents told their daughter of her adoption, she reacted harshly. The unexpected announcement threw her into rebellion, heavy drinking, and even rejection of her adopted family. I wanted to shield Isa from the hurt that led to that reaction. I also tried to protect myself against that kind of potential backlash. So, I'd break the news to Isa when she finished high school. At least that was my plan.

But then one day, a friend called, alerting me that Isa had privately questioned why I had not talked to her about her adoption. Fearing that my withholding of information from her might become an issue, I decided not to delay the conversation. This unfolded on a day when we were both at my workplace. I was in my office, and Isa was studying in another room. I grabbed Isa and suggested that we meet in the conference room. Looking back, that glassed-in meeting space—a fishbowl of a room, which employees frequently passed and peered into—may not have been the best venue for an intimate father/daughter conversation. But there we were. I leaned in close and let go of the story of how I became her father: how her birth mother, a longtime friend, had come to me saying she could not care for the child she was carrying and offering me the chance of adoption; the arduous adoption process; my fears that she might call her birth mother—whom Isa already knew. Over the speakerphone, she confirmed that she had only given Isa for adoption because she was not in a position to care for her. When I finished, my nerves were a hot mess. I looked my daughter in the eyes. How would she take it? Would this mark that lousy turn in our relationship that I had been fearing? I braced myself.

This was beyond doubt the most challenging episode of my journey with parenthood. But, for sure, there had been other trying moments. The first came long before Isa came along. I was in my early twenties and had just realized that I wanted a child. I could envision it all—cradling a baby, taking them to visit the family, teaching them what I knew about life. It didn't matter if it was a boy or a girl. I just felt deep inside that being a dad was part of my destiny. My thinking was inspired in part by the culture of my upbringing. Children and child-raising were a vital part of it. My brother, sister, and cousins all had kids. All up and down the neighborhood where I lived as a boy, kids were always playing on sidewalks and riding their bikes up and down the street.

Adoption was not new in my family. My African American grandfather and white grandmother adopted a son when they were in their fifties. My sister had also adopted a baby girl. Those examples gave me hope—and a kind of road map.

Still, I knew that my path to becoming a dad would be long, winding, and complicated. It was the early 2000s, and gay adoption was still fledgling. They didn't make it easy for a gay man in the middle of the Bible Belt to independently adopt a biracial child. (Almost twenty years after my experience, it is still hard for a gay couple to adopt in Tennessee.) Apart from the legal hurdles, there would probably be issues of social acceptance. I had every reason to be discouraged.

But I pushed on. At one point, I reached out to the only openly gay parent I knew of at the time—Rosie O'Donnell, the actress and television personality. She had adopted several children and was an outspoken advocate for gay adoption. Somehow, I got her number, and before I knew it, I was on the phone, peppering her with questions about adoption. She was encouraging and told me she would do all she could to help. Unfortunately, we lost contact somewhere along the way.

And then one day Alisa, a trusted friend, showed up at the apartment I shared with Adriene, my boyfriend at the time. In the course of our long and close friendship, I had confided many of my life ambitions to her, including my dream of parenthood. Her visit that day will always live big in my memories. She pulled up in her big, long, burgundy Suburban, rang the doorbell, sat down at our old, yellow fifties dining room table, and announced that she was pregnant. We congratulated her. She then acknowledged that she did not feel she was in a position to raise the baby. We knew the father was no longer in her life.

"Do y'all want to adopt?" she asked.

I stared at her, at first incredulous. Then I looked up and gave the Lord a thank-you. Deep inside I knew that the Universe was doing its work.

Isa's birth was a drama too. I guess all deliveries are. It started on a Monday in March of 2003, when Alisa called to tell me that her water had broken. From there, events happened so fast I can only recall the highlights. Alisa and I were in a car en route to Baptist Hospital in Nashville, where my mom had given birth to me. Then we were in the delivery room, with the medical team all in green scrubs. Suddenly, I was cutting the cord, barely holding on to my nerves. In the rush of things, I was overwhelmed with joy. Later, after they wheeled Alisa away, and I was alone with my daughter, a wave of anxiety swept in. What had I just done?

In a couple of days, we were home. I had to focus on the day-to-day demands of childcare—things like setting up the crib and stocking up on baby formula. My anxiety faded and was quickly replaced by the need to burp my daughter and change her diapers. In what seemed like a week, Isa went from four pounds to eight and then twelve. I understood that this moment of all-out focus would probably be for around the first year. So, I needed to slow down and enjoy it.

Another moment of anxiety came when Isa was a toddler. I had been spending a lot of time at home with her. But I knew I needed to get back into work heavily. So, I decided to start her in a daycare facility. When the day came, I remember feeling like this was going to be hard. We'd become inseparable, and now I had to leave her with these people she didn't know and she was going to cry.

Instead, she was all smiles, ready to go. It was me who cried. It was then that I realized this little child was independent. She could do things on her own.

Now, years later, sitting across from Isa in the conference room, I realized these flashbacks were not merely random parenting scenes. In each episode, I had started with anxious questions. Could I have a child at all? Could I raise a baby? Could I leave my precious daughter in the care of others? And in each case, my fears would turn out to be unwarranted. Of course, I could have a child. Sure, I could raise her. And no, I did not have to be with her 24-7. She would be fine under the watchful eyes of others.

That's when it hit me that this moment of tension would also pass. So, there I was, face to face with the person I cherished most. After watching me cry and then listening carefully, Isa let her tears flow too. When things calmed, she explained that she had figured out some time back that she was adopted. She knew that her birth mom and I were white, so chances were low that I could be her birth father. She understood and embraced the love I had given her over the years. She was just waiting for me to tell her. She accepted my apology for not telling her sooner. Our emotional exchange that afternoon gave way to a new phase of our relationship. The fear I had of rejection, love loss, or separation seemed to disintegrate. I felt thankful that I had "the Adoption Talk." From that point forward, our bond was strengthened. We could be honest and open about everything, including the hard stuff.

# THE ABCs OF BEING A GOOD PARENT

Many people have asked about my approach to parenting. Especially since Isa has grown to become a poised young lady, I guess what they're asking is how I pulled it off. In many ways, parenting a child as a gay dad is probably not much different from any other parenting. If you do it right, it's a mix of work, love, teaching, sharing, and guiding. Like most parents, I viewed myself mostly as the human who would help my kid get to where she was going. But of course, my parenting style is probably unique or at least different from most in a few ways.

For one thing, I made up my own creed or guidelines about what it takes to be a good father. Unlike many new parents, I did not have a mom and dad passing on tips or advice about being a good dad. My dad was long since gone. While Marilyn, my mom, took some interest in being a grandparent to Isa, she was not there to show me how to burp a baby, change a diaper, or stuff like that. In many ways, my parents served as examples of what not to do. I recognized the importance of being present in my daughter's life in ways that my mother had not been in mine. I understood the need to be truthful as my father had not been with me.

**I MADE UP MY OWN CREED OR GUIDELINES ABOUT WHAT IT TAKES TO BE A GOOD FATHER.**

Instead, in figuring out the best approach to parenting, I had relied on a mix of instinct and insights from observing other parent/child interactions. As a kid, I had watched the positive reinforcement that the parents of my friends Vafa and Safa had given them. I had seen other parents constantly berating their kids and made a mental note to steer away from that kind of negativity. I even took tips from Mama, the blue-haired matriarch in the sitcom *Mama's Family*. Perhaps above all, I looked into myself and channeled the dad in my heart about what was right and what was not. Out of all that, Elliott's unwritten rules about parenting took shape. It was part common sense and part daily improvising.

One thing I was clear about: I did not feel I had to sacrifice the ambition of being a boss for the dream of being a parent. I could be a successful leader at my company and a good dad at the same time. I just needed to work out a strategy for balancing both.

Another goal I established early was for Isa to experience the joys of life in the way that I did. I know many parents who feel that they have to stay home when they have kids and get fat and depressed. I call BS on that. When Isa was just a year old, I took her on a trip to Vegas. Since then, we have been to many spectacular events together—from concerts to a book party with Michelle Obama, as well as a trip to Europe. Just as I have gone about trying to live a full life, I've tried to make my daughter a part of it.

Discipline is another area where my approach differs from that of many parents. I believe that when children make mistakes, their parents should punish them. Sometimes, a reprimand is enough. At other times, restricting or revoking privileges becomes necessary. And then there are those rare infractions that call for a whupping. When I met with Isa's teachers, I informed them that I was not like many of the typical wealthy white parents at her school. When they are informed of issues with their kids, many of them instinctively jump into a defensive mode, saying they can't believe their offspring did anything terrible. If Susie or Mary acted up, I am not going to say I hope they are doing okay and we'll work through these things. I am not that parent. I think if my daughter does something she's not supposed to, she has to face judgment. And depending on the issue, I'm probably not just taking her phone away for only an hour or a day. I resort to measures others might regard as extreme.

Fortunately, 95 percent of the time, Isa has been a good student, an obedient and focused daughter, and a real angel. But there were occasional slipups. One came when she was in fourth or fifth grade. They called me from school and said that Isa was caught stealing a pencil and an eraser. I understood the principle involved here, that if she starts with this, what does that mean? And where's it going? I raised the issue with her. "No, sir," she said. "I did not do that." "Okay, I'm going to trust you. If I find out differently, it's going to be a different scenario." Maybe two days passed, and they called me again and said that she took somebody's ruler. I remember going into her bedroom. "Isa, I'm going to give you one opportunity to tell me the truth, and if you don't tell me the truth, you're going to get spanked." Again, she denied everything. I then looked in her backpack and found everything, so I spanked her.

On another occasion, when Isa did something wrong, I took her phone away for a year. At a later time, she had another rough spell and without a qualm, I took the Mercedes I had given her for her sixteenth birthday and sold it. In other words, I am strict. It's no wonder that Isa has said as a parent, I am more like an African American mama than a white dad. I am okay with that.

Of course, the positive experiences Isa and I have shared far outweighed the tense ones. My devotion to nurturing and growing together came before everything. I placed particular value on our regular father/daughter rituals. Every Wednesday, almost without fail, we had a breakfast date at the Waffle House. There were regular mani/pedi visits too.

Through it all—the celebrations, everyday life together, and even the punishments—I learned one big thing: that the love a parent has for his child is like no other love. Spouses and life partners have

**AS A PARENT, YOU TAKE FULL RESPONSIBILITY FOR ANOTHER PERSON'S LIFE.**

a special bond, of course. But as a parent, you take full responsibility for another person's life. It's an incredible experience, a gift. I am grateful to have it. I have no idea what my life would have been like without Isa.

# BUILDING MY FAMILY

As precious as my life with Isa was, with the passing of years, I was missing a partner in my life. I had decent experiences dating. But I had not met The One. And then one day in 2015, I came across a post by Donte on Facebook. We had a mutual FB friend who neither of us had actually met. It was a wonderful match from the start. We had so many critical things in common: ambition to build something bigger than us; an understanding of the importance of commitment in a relationship; a sense of adventure. It didn't hurt that he was extremely handsome. There was distance between us. He was based in New York and I in Nashville. We were Facebook friends for a couple of months when he posted a memory of his boyfriend passing a year earlier. It touched me because of my experience with losing a loved one. I reached out to him to offer advice on how to deal with grief.

I called him, and we had a very good back and forth. Other great conversations followed. Finally, we decided we needed to meet in person. Within a few days, I was on a plane to New York.

The dating was long-distance at first. We'd meet in Atlanta, New York, or Nashville. After around seven months, Donte decided to make the leap and move to Nashville.

Until then, I had no intentions of ever getting married. But as our love crystallized, I told my mom, "I'm going to marry him." A year and a half after meeting, we gathered our friends and family and exchanged vows in a poignant ceremony at the Bridge Building in Nashville. Unfortunately, my mom had died shortly before the engagement.

As Isa matured, I appreciated the importance of having other adults engaged in her upbringing. Fortunately, she bonded easily with Donte. He's younger than me so the smaller age difference between them made communication easy. He also had a good relationship with a niece around Isa's age, so he understood the issues facing teenage girls. Besides Donte, Debbie, a close friend of mine, took on the role of grandmother to Isa. She's the mother of Adriene, the guy I was dating when Isa was born. While he dropped out of my life, she remained in it. She has cared for Isa as her own kin. An African American matriarch, she is a key member of our extended family and very old school. She has been hands on in Isa's upbringing. Isa goes to Debbie's house in Florida for Christmas and Easter and sometimes during the summer. My friends Kenya, Courtney, and others also played strong roles in helping to raise Isa. As African Americans, Debbie and others offered a world view that I, as a white man, could not. Together, we became the village that has raised Isa.

# CREATING YOUR OWN VISION BOARD

## EXERCISE FOUR:
### Live Up to Your Principles

My mother's life motto was to live so you don't have to explain.

What are the sayings or expressions that you live by?

This assignment is to collect images that reflect your guiding principles.

For some people one strong saying—such as do unto others as you would have them do unto you—rules above all. Others might have a set of principles that they live by.

For this part of your board, get some lettering and spell out the motto or mottoes that speak to you.

To make the board more visually alluring, sift through some magazines to find scenes that help illustrate your codes.

I suspect that for many, this may be one of the most important aspects of their board.

# CHAPTER FIVE

# LIVE SO YOU DON'T HAVE TO EXPLAIN

A call from my mom transformed my life—and hers. It happened when she was in her early sixties, and I was not quite thirty.

To appreciate the importance of the moment, a bit of history about my mom and our relationship might help. After I came along, Marilyn Holt's life was divided into three distinct phases. In the early years, she was a workaholic. She kept the same job as a medical transcriptionist at Tennessee Orthopedic Alliance for thirty years. She loved everything about that position: the daily grind, the doctors, and of course, the regular paycheck. She would toil nights, bring work home, and labor through many weekends. Throughout that period, she was mostly a shadow in my life and at family rituals. By the time I woke for breakfast and school, she had left for work. When she came home, she'd head to her room, read magazines, and eat Hershey's chocolate. My closeness to my dad compensated for her absence.

The second phase started with my parents' divorce. Even though she and my dad had long-standing issues, his affair with another woman and the breakup of the marriage took a devastating toll. In her early forties, overweight, and on her own for the first time, she fell into depression. Eventually, she threw herself into a remake, centered on weight loss at Jenny Craig. She also found a new love, a boyfriend. For what seemed like the longest time, she left me to fend for myself emotionally. Then, when I was in my late twenties, with a business and a family of my own, she turned back toward me. Part of the reason was probably that my daughter had come into the picture, and she wanted to be involved more in Christmases and Thanksgivings and child-raising in general. She wanted to be more engaged in my business too. I welcomed all that. I wanted her to be there.

My most vivid memories of Mom in those early years were captured in isolated flashbacks.

One was the Sunday church ritual. She would dress in her Sunday best, and then with my dad and me, pile into the car and head to our regular place of worship. Throughout the morning and up to the front door, the two of them would always be bickering about something. But once we slid into the pew, we were a picture of family church togetherness and calm. Afterward, we would pick up a chicken at Lee's restaurant. Mom would always get the breast; we would share whatever was left, and the bickering would start again. This kind of churchgoing ritual was pretty standard for Southern families.

What made our case remarkable was that the service was sandwiched between one long live-streaming argument. And I was in the back seat watching the drama.

Another memory was of Mom in full work mode. After the divorce, my parents split custody over me. On the days I was with her, Mom would pick me up from school to take me to her workplace. No sooner had I entered her car than she started laying down the rules: sit still, don't touch this, don't do that. And when we got to work, she'd drill down. Yes, ma'am; no, ma'am. Yes, sir; no, sir. Stay seated. Do not get up. She was very to the point. She concentrated with a laser beam on her work and kept at it until it was time to go home. I had known my mom was a workaholic, but this was the first time I witnessed just how driven she was.

A third important scene happened when I was in my early twenties. By that time, I had already decided that I would not get emotional support from family and so had to forge my own path, in terms of both work and my personal life. Sitting on my apartment's sofa, she burst into tears and told me how sorry she was for not being there for me after the divorce and my father's passing. She acknowledged that she had been going through emotional pain too. But she had deep regret about not giving me the attention I needed. I told her I understood. I forgave her.

For the longest time, I thought of these as disconnected vignettes of a mother-son relationship in the arc from childhood through early adulthood. Although my mom never sat down and taught principles—about God, work, or anything else—she had tried to lead by example. With time, I realized that embedded in each of these flashbacks were life lessons. No matter what is going on in your life, do the right thing by God and the Universe. Be disciplined and focused on your work. When you are wrong, own up to it. These were rules my mom lived by and that she wanted me to follow too. The most significant and impactful of those lessons would come out in full force later, during the third phase of her life.

# FIGHTING FOR LIFE

By the time Mom turned sixty, her health was fragile. She had diabetes and had suffered two heart attacks. She also had a long-term struggle with eating and weight gain. I moved her to an apartment in downtown Nashville. I wanted her to be closer to me and, more importantly, closer to the hospitals. She had stopped driving, and my brother, Matt, and I would visit her often, bringing food and sometimes cooking. Mom and I talked three times a day, mostly to chat and check in.

And then, a year after she had settled into her new home, the call came. I was in a meeting and missed it. But when I saw she had attempted to reach out, a feeling of dread came over me. It was a sensation that anyone who has cared for aging parents knows: the aching fear that this might be it.

Fortunately, she also called Matt, who was working with me. Her voice was too weak for him to grasp what she was saying entirely. But we both knew enough to recognize that this was a red alert. Matt arrived first. By the time I arrived, she was lying on the bed with her feet draped over the side. She tried to talk but what came out was incoherent. I recognized the signs. She was in the middle of a stroke. I laid my hand on her belly, holding her and telling her that it would be all right and reassuring her of how much we loved her. I couldn't help but wonder, was this another parental death?

With that scare, I decided to start a new phase of life for my mom and myself. Having lost one parent, I was determined to do all I could to help her through this and make the most of whatever remained of her life. I wanted to devote myself to her to make sure that I made my mother a priority. Fortunately, we had gotten to her in time. The recovery would be grueling, made more difficult by her initial resistance. But she pushed through it. I managed her rehabilitation, doctor's visits, and daily care. Among other things, I created a vision board with goals for her and hung it in her hospital room to give her something to look forward to.

Whenever she needed me, I did my best to be there. Once, when I was at my second home in Atlanta, Mom had a rough night with her medications and was just feeling bad. I left immediately and rushed back to my mom, surprising her when I showed up at her home. When I walked through her bedroom door, she jumped up with excitement and appreciation that I had driven from Atlanta to Nashville for her.

In that period of bonding, the value of our relationship quadrupled. Above all, I offered unconditional love, and she returned it. I started to feel her respect for who I was. She began to see I was more than just her son. Just as importantly, she began to see me as more than a gay man. She started to see all of me.

And in many ways, the person she saw was very much like her. We were both cursers and hotheaded. We were also overly emotional, caring, loving, nurturing, and sympathetic. We were givers and will always look to help someone in need. We both struggled with weight. The differences between us were apparent too. We viewed our family differently. She knew I could walk away when there was little to no value in a relationship. I am way more optimistic and more of a risk taker.

Taking on the caregiver role required making some crucial changes in my approach to managing the business. Up until then, I felt the need to be in control of every part of the company. With newfound responsibility for my mom, I knew I had to start delegating tasks to other managers. Fortunately, I had the right people in the right seats, starting with a top-notch director of operations and compliance director. I let them and others know that they needed to step up to the plate. And they did, with flying colors.

I had to make adaptations in my home life too. I probably took away some time from my daughter. I was transparent with her, telling her exactly what was going on and what to expect from me. I feel like I took time away from our relationship. I also laid out what I needed from her. With open and honest communication—the key to any relationship—it worked.

Throughout our years together and particularly in our period of intense bonding, my mom taught me valuable rules to live by. She exhibited the meaning of empathy, love for others, and compassion, as well as the values of sensitivity, vulnerability, and open and honest communication. She taught me why giving to others, and not expecting anything back from them, is essential. She taught me the value of a parent/child relationship and that you can be forgiven and given another chance, no matter what.

**SHE DRAMATIZED THE IMPORTANCE OF HER MOTTO: LIVE SO THAT YOU DON'T HAVE TO EXPLAIN.**

With her actions, she dramatized the importance of her motto: live so that you don't have to explain. In essence, she meant—do the right thing! It was something she had said since I was a kid, but mainly in this period, the message rang in my ear and resonated. Over time, it became the equivalent of having an angel on my shoulder. It was my constant reminder to live right and if I did, good things would happen and I would not have to explain myself out of a negative situation. This resonated with me. It aligned with my core beliefs and everything I had learned in the Christian school.

The differences between those who live so they don't have to explain and others are centered on truthfulness. It harkens back to the old saying that the truth will set you free. I adopted this way of thinking from my mom, and it became my mantra. I am a truth whisperer. That, in turn, has given me a positive force of energy that protects me. I claim this as a superpower.

As close and protective I was with my mom, I acknowledged that she was not perfect. When I was growing up, she was messy and not at all into house cleaning. She never cooked. Instead of family meals around the table, we lived off Taco Bell, fried chicken, and other stuff picked up from fast-food places. Her home life was disorganized.

Instead of critiquing her bad habits, I took them as examples of how to be better. I recognized the importance of having a clean home, so I would tidy up all the rooms. It's a habit I have kept up into adulthood. While my parents never had food around the house, I like to keep our pantry and refrigerator well stocked. In contrast to my mother, I often cook meals for myself and my family. In a way, doing these things is a deliberate attempt to create order in my own home where there was none in my parents' house. But it's also true that doing household chores brings me personal pleasure.

# RECONCILIATION AND FORGIVENESS

This period of bonding and family togetherness also helped me understand and forgive my father. It made me aware that I had also made mistakes in my relationship with him. Ten days before my dad died, we had gotten into an argument. I threw him up against the front door of our home. I would give anything to go back and change that. Just take those minutes and hug this man who helped create me. My father and I never talked about his affair, the divorce, or me being gay. After he passed, I felt robbed of those conversations.

On the one hand, I had not had the time to let him get to know the real me, all of me. On the other hand, I felt that he had not explained how he had been living. But with time, I was able to process all that and forgive him. One thing that helped was hearing stories from his friends and family about how much he loved me and talked about me. It was comforting to know that he still felt about me the way he did before the affair. Above all, I realized and accepted his humanness. He didn't know it all. Various insecurities and desires led him to make the decisions he made. Even in cases where the decisions were terrible, he meant no harm. In a sense, I was an innocent bystander.

Being able to forgive my dad helped lift the dark shadow that had hung over my life following my father's death. It also allowed me to have a new, positive relationship with him. Since that fateful day in 1996, when I returned home to find him dead, we have had many talks. I believe that he continues to protect and guide me.

> **BEING ABLE TO FORGIVE MY DAD HELPED LIFT THE DARK SHADOW THAT HAD HUNG OVER MY LIFE FOLLOWING MY FATHER'S DEATH.**

After overcoming a series of battles—with weight, heart issues, and depression among many others—my mom came to embrace life. She enjoyed spending time with me, Matt, and others and wanted to keep up her active life, including her roles as mother and grandmother. But a couple of years after the stroke, her many years of unhealthy living began to take their heavy toll.

In early spring of 2015, Mom's cardiologist let us know that her heart was working at 5 percent. He told us she had six months to live. We would spend every day of that period celebrating life. There was lots of talk about the past and the future, many dinners with friends and visits to the park. She watched her most beloved soap operas and ate chicken breast and all of her other favorite foods. She told me on numerous occasions that she was not ready to die. She did not want to leave me. I believed her. But I also knew it was too late.

In November of that year, while I was on a trip to Chicago with Donte, my godmother called to tell me that Mom was going to the hospital. We immediately headed back to Nashville. When we arrived, Mom was in the hospital unconscious. The nurse said she was sedated for comfort, but she was wide awake and feeling incredible the next morning. We talked for hours. That night she was transferred to a hospice where she would spend her last few days sedated. I got the call on November 10, 2015, that my mother had passed.

As I stood up to speak, I cried a river and then another one. At her funeral, I thanked her for all she had given me. I was grateful for lessons of everything from forgiveness to honoring family. What resonated above all was her exhortation to live so you don't have to explain.

# CREATING YOUR OWN VISION BOARD

## EXERCISE FIVE:
### A Portrait of Your Ideal Family

Close your eyes and imagine yourself stranded on a desert island. Make a list of the twelve people you would want to have with you. Many or all of them may be in your blood family. It may include partners or friends you have come to know and trust. It may also include persons you admire but do not know well: a work colleague, a neighbor, a workout buddy at the gym. Whoever it includes constitutes your dream family.

When I made my list, it included my mother and a couple of relatives. Of course, my husband and our daughter were there too. Several friends I had become close to over time were also part of it.

For this section of your vision board, collect images of you surrounded by pictures of the twelve people. This depiction of your chosen family is a powerful expression of who you are and who you aspire to be. It is also a reminder of who you feel comfortable calling in times of need. Save these images with the others you have gathered for your vision board.

# CHAPTER SIX
## THOUGHTS BECOME THINGS

A while back, in a vision board I created reflecting my hopes for the coming year, one image stood out. It was a photo of two toddlers, brown-skinned boys with curly hair and wide grins. They were probably brothers, perhaps twins. I had taken that photo from a magazine and included it on the board as an expression of a dream Donte and I had been harboring for a while—to become fathers again. We had not only determined that we wanted to be parents; we specifically hoped for twin boys. One reason that photo stood out is that it represented a pretty audacious dream. Even though adoption laws for gays have improved in some places, there are still restrictions. Surrogate parenthood was an option, but one that came with its own set of issues. If my husband and I could jump over those hurdles by some miracle, what were the odds that we would eventually be parents of two babies? Chances were slim. Even though I was aware that the odds were something of a fantasy, I also knew that nothing would happen unless I expressed my wish. Putting the picture of two kids on the vision board was the first step in advancing our dream. And every plan starts with the expression of a thought. I

**EVERY PLAN STARTS WITH THE EXPRESSION OF A THOUGHT.**

was anxious to see if the picture of the two boys could be transformed into a reality.

Ever since I was in my early twenties, I have used vision boards to help put faces and images to my wishes, dreams, and ambitions. Constructing the boards has become an annual ritual. Toward the end of every year, I make a trip to a Nashville arts store to buy poster boards, glue, magazines, and photos and then use them to compose a board of my visions. Of course, my dreams shift every year, and so do the images on my board. In 2018, I included the headline "Entrepreneur of the Year," reflecting a hope that I would be cited for achievements at MediCopy. I also included a smiling picture of Reba McEntire, one of my all-time favorite singers, someone whom I had dreams of befriending. The next year, my board featured a picture of a muscular male torso with the headline "Feel Good, Healthy Body." That reflected my goal of getting in better physical shape. I also included the headline "Inc. 5000," showing my hopes that MediCopy would be named in *Inc.* magazine's list of top growing businesses. There are some types of images that I include every year. Since the success of MediCopy is always one of my highest objectives, I frequently include scenes and headlines signifying business growth on my boards.

# THE SECRET OF THE SECRET

As crucial as the vision boards are, they are not sufficient in obtaining goals. I also regularly engage in other rituals to help me make my dreams come true. One of them is following the procedures prescribed in the book and movie *The Secret*. Rhonda Byrne, an internationally renowned spiritual guru, created these procedures and detailed them in the book and movie. Kristin, one of my dearest childhood friends, first recommended *The Secret* when I was in my late teens, and it has been like a Bible to me ever since. The formula of *The Secret* boils down to three simple steps: 1) Ask for the things you want; 2) Believe those things are attainable; 3) Prepare to receive what you ask for. This process of requesting, thinking, and receiving has become a daily ritual that I follow religiously. I have come to believe in it so passionately that I recommend *The Secret* to everyone I know. I keep copies of the book in my office and give them to all new employees. And whenever I pass on the gift, I explain how thoughts can become things and the critical role *The Secret* plays in that process.

While following the formula of *The Secret* plays a decisive role in realizing dreams, if you really want to achieve goals, more is needed. Having faith—and expressing that faith through prayer—is also vital. Many people—including most of those in my circle of friends—look to the traditional church as a place to go to express faith and commune with God. I understand and respect this. The church also played a central role in my upbringing. I went to a Christian school and church from pre-K until my parents' divorce. After that, my mother took me to a Presbyterian church. These days, when anyone asks what my faith or religion is, I identify as a Baptist. I have also attended different places of worship with my friends, including the Catholic church, the Baha'i Center, and others. I have learned a lot from observing and sharing in these approaches to religion. When I was a teen, the Baha'i faith spoke to me more than others. The fundamental teachings of the faith that attract me are God's oneness, the unity of religion, the unity of humankind, equality of men and women, elimination of all forms of prejudice, and independent investigation of truth. Some of these teachings have followed me throughout my life. In all of them—and in fact in the teaching of other religions I have been exposed to—I have found the message to be consistent. The keepers of the faith present the rules. If their followers adhere to those rules, the reward is eternal life in heaven.

Over the years, however, I have distanced myself from the organized church. The overall hypocrisy and views on the LGBTQ lifestyle became nonnegotiable negatives for me. Church attendance put me in uncomfortable and sometimes quite negative situations.

Still, having—and expressing—my faith regularly is one of the essential pillars of my life. I reaffirm my faith first thing every morning, without fail, by reciting the prayer of Jabez. The prayer in 1 Chronicles 4:10 in the Old Testament of the Bible goes like this:

*"Oh, that you would bless me and enlarge my territory! Let your hand be with me and keep me from harm so that I will be free from pain."*

The prayer, powerful in its directness and simplicity, has served as a spiritual anchor for me throughout my adult life. Like Jabez, the biblical character who first gave voice to the prayer, in reciting it, I am asking for four things: God's blessing, an expansion of my territory, the presence of God's hand, and His protection from harm.

Kristin, the friend who first taught me about *The Secret*, also introduced me to the prayer of Jabez. Through this prayer, I ask God and the Universe for anything—not just materialistic things. When

I say this prayer, I believe that God and the Universe are listening. As long as I am open to whatever they will give me, I have positive actions behind my intentions, and I am confident that I will receive those things.

Besides being instrumental in achieving goals, my faith has helped save me from many bad personal and professional situations. When the Holy Spirit, or God, speaks to me, sometimes it manifests itself through my gut. We all know this feeling. It surfaces most often when we are in right or wrong or angel and devil situations. Whenever I am in predicaments like that,

**PERHAPS MORE IMPORTANT THAN ASKING GOD TO HELP ME FULFILL MY DREAMS IS UNDERSTANDING THAT EVERY DAY GOD IS GOING TO USE ME THE WAY HE WANTS TO USE ME.**

I think of the Bible and the Ten Commandments. I can't help but think how simple it would have been just to have one commandment that stated, "Do the RIGHT thing."

Perhaps more important than asking God to help me fulfill my dreams is understanding that every day God is going to use me the way He wants to use me. And I'm open and receptive to being used. This involves surrendering and being vulnerable to God and the Universe. I think many people don't have enough faith or belief to surrender in that way.

When I give in to the will of God and the Universe, I experience occasions in which they have plans for me that are different from what I imagined or hoped for. Just because I think and believe in something doesn't mean it's the right thing for me. At times, when I express a wish through prayer, God has said, "Hey, hold up; let's slow your roll.

Let's look at it this way." Or "That's not what I have in mind for you." My plans take a life of their own. That life of their own comes from having faith. Faith is what you put into it. The way God wants it to be is what comes out.

The final—and perhaps most important—step I take to fulfill my dreams is to work for them. While I believe that good things will come to those who live correctly, I also think putting the work in is necessary. For me, that has meant putting in the time to build a business. It has meant devoting attention to my husband and daughter. It's also meant creating things such as this book, a podcast, and other projects.

# HOW MY THOUGHTS HAVE BECOME THINGS

My life has become proof of the power of thoughts becoming things.

Like most people, I start by expressing big dreams with thoughts to myself. Way back when I was a teenager working at the Tennessee Orthopedic Alliance, I saw an opportunity to create a business in health information management. A few years later, the idea of becoming a father came to me. Years later, I began thinking that my life would be better if I had a committed partner. For instance, I began working toward transforming these dreams into a reality. With time, prayer, work, and focus, MediCopy launched and snowballed. My daughter came into my life. I met the partner of my dreams, and we are now building our lives and dreams together.

Other less lofty thoughts I have had also became realities. In 2018, the year I included Michelle Obama on my vision board, I had the chance to meet with her twice. The first time was in Chicago at the launch of her tour for her book *Becoming*. The second was at the end of that tour in Nashville. I invited Isa, Donte, and a few friends to a private party she held. And my dream of being included in *Inc.'s* top 5000 fastest-growing companies has come true as well. Every year for the past eight years, *Inc.* has included MediCopy on the list.

Some of my dreams have not come true quite yet. My hopes of meeting Reba McEntire and becoming friends with her hasn't happened yet. It almost did. One day a friend called me up and told me that she was sitting right next to him in a restaurant. I hightailed it over there. But when I came within a few feet of her, I realized it was not the right occasion. But I know one day Reba and I will meet. Before the COVID-19 pandemic hit, I had plans of making major trips with my family. The pandemic kept us close to home. In such cases, I have accepted that God had other plans for me. The time will come for us to explore new destinations.

But the truth is that in some way, every hope I have comes true. It may not happen in the time frame I expected or in quite the way I envisioned, but it happens. I don't know if it's because I have so much faith or know that everything happens for a reason. And so, if something doesn't come my way as I imagined, I accept that what happens is how it was meant to be.

By all accounts, the dream Donte and I had of becoming fathers was meant to be. When we first became a couple, we talked for hours about having kids. Finally, one day I said, "Okay, when will we start doing something about it?" With that, we opted instead of adoption to start the surrogacy process. At the time of this book's writing, we are working with a great agency and have fifteen healthy embryos to choose from. Next, we're moving into the therapeutic phase. We will select two surrogates. We will swing it so they will be pregnant about thirty days apart. One surrogate could be in California and the other in New York; we just don't know yet. It looks like we're headed toward having two boys by the fall of 2021.

We look forward to expanding our family and sharing that unique love parents have for their children.

What started as a thought—as Donte and me fantasizing about becoming fathers of two boys—is well on its way to becoming a thing.

# CREATING YOUR OWN VISION BOARD

## EXERCISE SIX:
### Make Your Thoughts Become Things

To prepare for this section of your vision board, start by dreaming big about your ambitions, both personal and professional. Do you want to own your own home or car? Do you have a goal to own a business? Is having children and a family in your plans? Comb through magazines for photographs that represent all of these—and any other dreams you have—and compose a board of them.

This part of your board could also have images of the steps you need to achieve those goals. If owning a car is one of your dreams, for example, an image of someone depositing money in a bank may be appropriate as a visualization of what it might take to make that dream a reality.

Seeing these images on a regular basis on your board will help your thoughts become things.

# CHAPTER SEVEN
# BE SUCCESSFUL
## MY FIRST $1,000,000

**M**y journey to becoming a Bald Bearded Boss started with a single copy machine. It was a Hewlett Packard that printed twelve pages a minute. I used it to copy medical records for the Tennessee Orthopedic Alliance, my first—and for a while only—client. I placed the printer on a corner of a glass dining room table in my two-bedroom apartment. That table constituted my office. This was how MediCopy started. I made around $400 a week. It was about as hardscrabble a beginning as they come. But it was terrific. At twenty-one, I was the owner of my own business.

Twenty-one years later, MediCopy's staff has ballooned to over two hundred employees. The company has over four thousand clients, including some in just about every state of the US. Our Nashville office sprawls over twelve thousand square feet on the top floor of a swanky modern building. In 2021, for the eighth straight year, MediCopy was named to the Inc. 5000—the list of the fastest-growing midsize companies in the US. Earnings are around $25 million a year. Also in 2021, the company was valued at between $70 and $100 million.

Early on, I developed a formula for my earnings. I worked it out—back in May 2000—and I called my mom to tell her I'd just made $1,500 for an hour's work. "That's nice, honey," she said, apparently bemused. "No," I answered, "I don't think you understand. If I do this forty hours a week, I'll make more than $60,000." I still use the formula more than twenty years later, and I make $400,000 a week.

How did my business evolve from a bare-bones start-up to a robust, midsize, nationally recognized enterprise? I'd like to say that it was all part of a grand master plan. But it wasn't. It's true that since childhood, I had harbored a dream of being the boss of my own company. At five years old, I sat at my dad's desk, arranging papers into neat stacks. My original goal was modest: to make $50,000 a year. That was about what my mother earned, and she seemed pretty rich. If I could equal that, I thought, I'd be wealthy too.

But MediCopy grew organically, rising one day and one prayer at a time. As an owner, I had to continually seek out opportunities and take advantage of them. I made a fair share of mistakes and tried to learn from them. I had good fortune, including one unexpected event that would triple the company's revenues. Over time, I developed and followed a few business guidelines. They started as basic common-sense rules and eventually evolved into MediCopy's core values. They have proven key to the company's success.

# FIRST RULE: DEVOTE 200 PERCENT TO THE BUSINESS.

Particularly in the early phase, owners have to put all they have—from finances, mental acumen, and labor—toward making the company work. This all-in attitude is the cardinal rule for start-up entrepreneurs. It applied to me too. For me, MediCopy was a new love, a passion. From early on, it defined who I was. I threw everything I had into it. I bought the Hewlett Packard copy machine with a $500 gift card I got by signing up for an AOL account. I acquired a laptop by convincing a couple I knew to charge it on their Dell credit card. I made the $24 monthly payments. I made an advertising brochure using Word Perfect. I typed in the text, cut images with scissors, and pasted them on. I then sent it to Kinko's, where they printed it on résumé paper. Money was so tight at first that it did not cover my bills, so I took a second job making cookies in a bakery. At first, I did everything on my own. I had to. That meant workdays that stretched from the wee hours until very late at night. For a while, I could not pay myself a salary. I survived on the basics.

**MONEY WAS SO TIGHT AT FIRST THAT IT DID NOT COVER MY BILLS, SO I TOOK A SECOND JOB MAKING COOKIES IN A BAKERY.**

# SECOND RULE: BUILD TRUST WITH CLIENTS.

I started growing a customer base by making door-to-door sales in the same building where TOA was located. I then drove around Nashville in my 1996 hunter-green Eddie Bauer Ford Explorer. And eventually, I started canvassing businesses in the rest of Tennessee, searching out companies that needed a release-of-health-information service for their medical records.

I touted my experience—ongoing work with TOA and a background in maintaining medical records since I was fifteen. The most vital part of my pitch was honesty and openness about what I could do. I pledged to communicate and be available for my clients' needs. I also conscientiously kept up my end of the agreement. I had memories of my father's false promises on what he could deliver and did not want to repeat that habit. I drove that old truck from client to client, seeking out new clients and servicing existing ones, until it had almost three hundred thousand miles on it. My salesmanship worked. Within a year, I took on several doctors' offices in the TOA building. Then came Nashville Ear, Nose and Throat; Neurosurgical Associates; and Physicians and Surgeons in Pulaski, Tennessee. More than two decades later, some of the original clients are still with us.

## THIRD RULE: NURTURE YOUR EMPLOYEES.

After a year, I hired my first employee, my brother's ex-wife. I needed someone to go to doctors' offices in the south Tennessee area, and that's where she lived. She worked one day a week, on Fridays. Soon after, I brought on Courtney, who had been my best friend for years. He also made sales in Chattanooga and northern Georgia, and eventually Knoxville. Bit by bit, I added other staff members. From the beginning, I made clear what I expected in terms of work ethic. I could not put up with whiners or naysayers. But I also emphasized how much I valued the professional growth of anyone who came to work for me. I knew I had to lead by example. To do that, I had to work on myself and on how to set the best example. I also worked at responding to my employees' needs and investing in them and their careers. When they faced health complications or family issues, for instance, I always encouraged them to take the time to address those needs.

## FOURTH RULE: STAND OUT FROM THE COMPETITION.

Early on, I understood what MediCopy could offer that similar companies don't: its own personality. Other businesses don't take the time to create their aura. We do. Our employees have developed particular traits, starting with honesty, openness, and a commitment to grow. They pass those characteristics on to coworkers. Our clients are attracted to that. They understand that we're as committed to their success as we are to our own. We back up that optimistic spirit in concrete ways. We do things faster. We have a two-day turn-around time and excellent customer service. Since the beginning, our customer reviews have acknowledged that. On Google, we're number one among our competitors.

# TRANSFORMATIONAL EVENTS

Two significant occurrences contributed to MediCopy's surge of growth. The first was the introduction of electronic medical records in 2009 and 2010. As a company that had focused solely on copying and scanning paper records, I thought this would be our death knell. It turned out to be our salvation. With electronic records, we gained the capacity to log into our clients' systems without leaving the office in Nashville. We didn't need boots on the ground in Knoxville, Chattanooga, or any other city. We were able to go nationwide from our home base. We amassed clients in every corner of the US, from Washington, DC, to Los Angeles. The switch to electronic records helped the company triple in size between 2010 and 2020.

The second event was my decision to build a team of senior managers and delegate as many responsibilities as possible. I hired an HR manager, a director of compliance, a director of IT and health information services, and other top-tier staff. As a business owner who had gotten used to controlling everything, this step was a hard one for me at first. With time, I grasped the wisdom of getting rid of duties that I didn't want to do and giving them to someone else. Once the management team was up and running, they relieved me of things I felt they could do better. I didn't want to know anything about compliance; I wanted to send that to my director. I didn't want employees calling me if their paycheck was wrong or they wanted to update their 401(k); my director of HR or his assistant could handle those issues.

I created the new management team as a result of discussions I had at the Entrepreneur Organization. EO is a worldwide organization of entrepreneurs that meets once a month in a forum. There are also local chapters that gather regularly, sometimes in person and sometimes via Zoom. The conversations are about payroll, management issues, growing a business, and other things entrepreneurs don't feel they can talk about with their spouses, family, or friends. I joined EO in 2010 at the suggestion of a business associate. Several other members pressed the importance of delegation. I took heed.

Once the managers took charge, I pivoted my focus to the things I did best. Charting the future of the company was one of them. Typically, I like to stay two and three years ahead of current trends. I have to be focused on what's happening politically. I also have to stay informed about the laws introduced both federally and statewide that might affect the business.

It also allowed me to refine the guiding rules that helped MediCopy get its start. As the company prospered, I no longer needed to follow rule number one and devote 24-7 to working in the business. Instead, I could work on the business. But the emphases I established early—on client building and nurturing employees—were still as relevant as ever. Using those focuses as a basis, I worked on articulating our core values and assuring that they are part of the day-to-day operations at MediCopy.

# OUR GUIDING VALUES

The company's first core value is to maintain 100 percent accountability. I always tell employees that if we hire them for a position, we want it to be their position. We don't micromanage people. We train employees for six weeks. They will have a support team. They will be able to reach out to me if they need anything. But they own their jobs.

Our second value: embrace work/life balance. We want employees to work forty hours and to be 100 percent committed to their work during that time. They should then get out and enjoy their families, crafts or hobbies, or whatever they want to do.

Another significant value is donating time and resources. I like to give—and for the company to do so as well—whether it's money or time. As a staff, we have built houses and playgrounds. We serve at the Nashville Rescue Mission. On one occasion, they needed water, so we sent three thousand bottles. We're continually doing something to give back to the community because it's the right thing to do.

Fourth, we believe MediCopy employees should have continued personal and professional growth. I've never hired a manager or director externally. I promote from within the company. One example is Morgan,

**I'VE NEVER HIRED A MANAGER OR DIRECTOR EXTERNALLY. I PROMOTE FROM WITHIN THE COMPANY.**

a woman who first worked as a front-desk receptionist and in the mailroom. She's now our director of client engagement. I want employees to work their way up the same way I did. One advantage of this approach is that when someone asks employees a question, they can get an answer rather than being referred to someone else.

On the personal growth part, I also challenge every one of my employees to create a vision board. I give anybody who creates one eight hours of paid time off, and I reimburse them for their supplies. The panels are judged in a competition. The first-place winner wins a week off work, second place, three days off work, and third place, two days off work.

The reason I encourage vision boards is to get them in the spirit of thinking about or visualizing what they want for the next twelve or eighteen months of their lives. Those dreams can be anything—a house, time with family, a better connection with God or the Universe, or whatever it may be. I'm paying them eight hours to build a vision for their next year. It has been a blessing to see the things that come over vision boards. Whatever their vision might be, they're going to step their game up at work to try to make it happen. In the end, we all win because now the employees are doing their best to try to get that promotion and raise and work toward their vision.

Our last core value is yield quality above quantity. We all have production goals at MediCopy. An employee might have a goal of seventy-five. But I'll tell them I'd rather they do half of that and make it 100 percent correct than push out substandard work.

Just as it is crucial to follow these core values, it is also a top priority for me to maintain the right culture at the business. Most people look at culture as having gumball machines, snacks, and beer on tap. But that's not culture to me. For me, one big thing culture means is assuring that we're a diverse group. I have built a management team that is 60 percent African American or LGBTQ. It also means maintaining a staff that is 77 percent women and 50 percent people of color. Another important thing is making sure there are no wage gaps between men and women. I also want to ensure that we're not paying white people more or vice versa. This is not about checking diversity boxes. I'm hiring badass people who are working their tails off and at the same time growing personally and professionally. They honor the same values that I do. And for that, they're rewarded.

I measure the success of our approach in a couple of ways. First, by how well we grow and keep our client base. Second, by how good we are at retaining our employees. Our turnover rate is less than 3 percent. Our client retention rate is steady at 99 percent, and our reviews are stellar and dominate the competition. In other words, almost no one leaves the company, neither clients nor employees. That tells me that we're doing something right. And as long as that's the case, I am driven to keep moving forward.

# CREATING YOUR OWN VISION BOARD

## EXERCISE SEVEN:
### Depicting Your Own Version of Success

For me, making my first million dollars was one clear sign of success, a real hallelujah moment. In what ways can success in your life be measured? Perhaps your yardstick is monetary. It could be spiritual, such as gaining peace of mind. It could also be physical, such as acquiring a better physique through exercise. Or it could be a combination of all these and other things.

Collect your own images of success to include in your vision board. Be bold and imaginative. This board is clearly one that should be put in a place of prominence. It will remind you of what you want to accomplish.

# CHAPTER EIGHT

# BE SELFISH

## MAKING TIME FOR YOURSELF

I f you ask a group of people the time of day they love best, many will answer five in the evening. For lots of folks, that's unwind time, the end of the workday, and the beginning of Happy Hour. Others may say dinnertime—the period of sitting around a table with family and good food. And then there are night owls who relish late-night adventures. At different phases, I have fallen into each of these groups.

Over time, four-thirty in the morning has become my favorite hour. That's when I make ninety minutes of space for myself. My family is usually sleeping, so the house is calm and dark. Fresh out of bed, I start the day by giving thanks to God and the Universe. Then comes exercise. In the winter months, that means an hour or so on my Peloton or treadmill. Finally, I meditate. By dawn, I will be sitting upright, crossed-legged, engaged in a guided meditation. I follow the instructor through the standard drill: controlling my breathing, taking a head-to-toe check of my body, then a mental focus on a theme such as faith, forgiveness, or stress. During a session centered on gratitude, I pictured my mother, then my father, sitting across from me. I expressed thanks to both for all they did for me. In the spring and summer months, when the weather is mild, my exercise consists of walking or jogging through a park near my home. All the while, I soak in nature and converse with God.

Of course, there is something selfish about taking this time for myself. I have come to accept it as a healthy kind of selfishness. It grounds and humbles me. I use this period to draw energy from God, from the Universe, and from within myself. And that renewed spirit reminds me that there is something out there that is way bigger than me, a driving force that inspires every decision and every move I make. Besides praying, meditating, and working up a sweat, as the morning moves into dawn, I begin visualizing how I want the day to play out both personally and professionally. Setting aside this kind of time is something everyone should do. It doesn't have to be at the crack of dawn. Most people like to reserve early mornings for sleep. Nor does it have to be a daily practice. Two or three times a week might be enough. But creating mental space for yourself somewhere can only be beneficial.

Those morning interludes set the tone for everything that happens for the rest of the day. They usually take me straight into a busy daily schedule. There's breakfast with my family, which is often oatmeal and fruit. Then coffee on the porch with my husband. A sales call with a potential client. Meetings with MediCopy managers. That brings me to lunch, which I usually share with the family. Business meetings follow that, and then family dinner. At night, I take a bit more time alone. I start with ten minutes on social media and then read a book. Each of these activities brings its kind of pleasure. I repeat them daily—though I don't do business calls on weekends.

In the arc of the fifteen or so years that I have been starting my day in this way, my mental focus during those early mornings has shifted from one major issue that is affecting me to another. In the infancy years of MediCopy, I concentrated on addressing my self-doubt and insecurities. I had persistent questions about my capabilities as a business owner. Having my own company had been my dream, but I wondered whether I could do it when the moment came. Particularly since I was starting with nothing, I had to earn respect from my employees. To do that, I had to start believing in myself. Eventually, with the guidance of God and the Universe, I was able to conquer those doubts. What ultimately helped was getting to the place where I could put myself in God's hands and allow Him to use me for whatever purpose He feels best. And with that awakening, I realized that I had what it takes to lead a company. I could grow from nothing to this. I realized that I was doing things that no one else was doing. And as I continued to accept that God was using me for positive good, my perspective changed. I accepted that I was becoming who I was meant to be. I said to myself, "Oh, this is who I was sitting at my dad's desk. It was this person I am today that I was envisioning." Taking that early morning time for myself was critical to making that journey from insecurity to confidence.

With this newfound sense of purpose and assurance, my

**TAKING THAT EARLY MORNING TIME FOR MYSELF WAS CRITICAL TO MAKING THAT JOURNEY FROM INSECURITY TO CONFIDENCE.**

concentration shifted from wondering whether I could do things to figuring out the best and most efficient way to get them done. I gained a sense of how to make priorities and the positive energy to accomplish must-do action items. The leadership of MediCopy was my prime concern. I recognized and accepted that I had a company with over two hundred employees who depend on me. Wherever there were opportunities to bring a positive impact, I would readily engage in them.

For years, much of my mental energy was spent on how to grow the business. I was continually looking for ways to expand our client base or the services we offered existing clients. During my morning reflections—and also when I was on vacations—lots of great ideas flowed. And when I got to the office, my operations director or director of accounting would ask, "Oh Lord, what's he got now?" They always knew I would have a to-do list of things to be changed or updated or some other bright ideas.

My commitment to bringing positive change has, in turn, given me the ability to know what things are not possible. I have learned to say no to anything that does not bring good energy, value, or satisfaction. In business, that has sometimes meant firing employees who could not obtain a positive work experience. As someone who believes in nurturing and empowering my staff, dismissing them was not something I took lightly. I always tried to address any issues that kept employees from performing. But when a resolution was not possible, I had no problems with termination. At times, I have also had to get rid of clients whose values did not align with ours. While never easy, cutting ties with them sometimes seemed like the best solution.

The ability and need to immediately reject negative behavior have affected my personal life too. It has made me conservative about how I spend my time. Whether it be family and friends inviting me to a function or listening to a friend or family member complain on the phone—I have guarded my heart and time. I value my friends, but I don't devote much time to their social endeavors. If there's a celebration and a milestone for someone, I'll be there to support that. But if they invite me to a casual gathering, I'll usually say no respectfully. Instead, I use my energy on things that I'm sure I am going to enjoy and not regret. And those moments and experiences of joy are essential for me.

## A NEW PATH FORWARD

With the business's success and my decision to delegate authority for running it to senior managers, my predawn thoughts have turned to how to bring value to the rest of my life. Letting go of control of various aspects of the business has been tough emotionally, but it has allowed me to redirect my energy to improving myself and being there more for my loved ones. Up until 2014, I had submerged myself in work. When Marilyn, my mother, had a stroke and a heart attack, they told her she had six months to live. I immediately took time off to spend with her. Although this may seem like it was not "me" time, it was. I knew Mom and I had a limited amount of time to spend together. I wanted and needed the closure that I did not get with my dad's death. So, I took leave for that. That break from routine allowed me to stop and say, "Okay, let me reflect on this. What's going on? What's God trying to tell me? What's the Universe telling me?" I have become acutely aware of the various ways that God communicates. If I don't listen closely, I can become like the rest of these fools out here, just wandering like zombies through life. If I sense that God is sending a message, I turn my ears in that direction. I then take heed by aborting the mission, changing the route or the date, upgrading, or doing whatever else I need to do.

My mother's subsequent passing made me realize that I should back away some from work and turn my attention elsewhere. One direction I turned was inward—on my health. Part of my longtime insecurity has centered on my body image and, in particular, on my weight. I have been overweight since I was twelve, and that is still a daily struggle. Am I happy with myself? Yes. Do I love myself? Yes. Do I want to be thirty pounds lighter? Yes. After years of dieting, jogging, and exercise, I have come to understand that my approach to addressing my weight issue has been off base. Instead of the goal of being skinny, I should be concentrating on being healthy. I've also realized that this is who I am, and my weight is just a piece of me, just like being gay or being a boss are also parts of me. That realization has helped me change the focus on my weight and the way I look. "Hold on," I told myself. "How about concentrating on being healthy and not slim?" My early morning meditation interludes proved instrumental in helping me arrive at this level of self-awareness.

Another direction I pivoted toward was my family, our future, and the next chapter of our lives. I felt the responsibility to provide for them, not just for the present, but for the future. Part of my mission has become to create experiences for us. When I was a child and adolescent, my parents were too busy making a living to think much about building the kinds of events we could treasure. There were no trips to Florida, New York, or much of anywhere else. I have taken it upon myself to create those kinds of memorable moments for me and my family. This wish to make lasting experiences for the family started

*I HAVE TAKEN IT UPON MYSELF TO CREATE THOSE KINDS OF MEMORABLE MOMENTS FOR ME AND MY FAMILY.*

when my daughter was only a year old and I took her to Las Vegas on vacation. Since then, we have stepped up our game with holidays to Europe, the Caribbean, and various corners of the US.

My engagement to Donte was an event that will be forever etched in both our minds. For his first birthday after we became a couple, we flew to St. Thomas. We stayed at the Ritz Carlton—a breathtaking hotel in the picture-perfect Cape Hatteras part of that Caribbean Island. Without Donte's knowledge, I had arranged an engagement dinner on the property. Set in a private gazebo, with a violin player and photographer, it was about as romantic an occasion as you can imagine. At an agreed-upon moment, one of the waiters came up and pretended that he had a package for Donte from the hotel. The box actually contained a ring of black diamonds that I had bought seven months earlier at a jeweler in Nashville. And with that, I asked him to marry me.

Of course, you don't have to go to an island to create a memorable experience. Our wedding—another spectacular event—took place not too far from our home, in downtown Nashville, at the Bridge Building—a riverfront venue with a spectacular view of the city. The occasion, in December 2016, extended over an evening and late into a night in three different settings. We started with cocktails in an open-air tent, then moved everyone inside the building for dinner. From there, we returned to the rooftop, which was decorated all in white for the ceremony. For the rooftop reception, they transformed the space into an elegant club atmosphere, complete with a crazy chandelier that they specially made for us. They had several cool bars up there too.

Music is vital to both of us, so we designed our playlist—twenty hours of tunes—for the DJ. The soundtrack of that evening, composed of all Donte's and my favorite songs, still rings in my ears. The musical highlight was pop singer Kylie Minogue's rendition of "I Should Be So Lucky." *Out & About Nashville*, our local LGBTQ magazine, called the event "The Gay Wedding of the Year." With our union, I had that feeling—one that I hadn't had since Isa was born—of overwhelming joy being with someone else you want to protect, that you want to love for the rest of your life.

One big lesson of the COVID-19 pandemic is that it's unnecessary to be extravagant or even leave home to create the type of special moments that stay with you. During the pandemic period, I worked from home. Isa, my daughter, was mostly in small classes at home too. That year of sheltering in place gave us a lot of time in the house at the same time. In those twelve months, we added the equivalent of five years to our experience together. I was not just seeing her when she got home from school for five minutes before she showered and did homework, ate dinner, and went to bed. We have breakfast together, we talk about what college will look like, and I don't mean just now and again, but every day. I let her make her own choices about college, her own decisions, about whatever it may be because I want it to be on her, not that she was forced to do something.

One subject we have talked about is race. Isa has helped me understand that even though I am married to an African American man and have a biracial daughter, I still need to learn more about racial issues. This period has given me confirmation and trust in Isa. I know she still might make silly decisions. And if she does, I will undoubtedly get onto her about them. But I'm going to let her go into the world knowing that she will make every effort to be the right person and do the right thing.

My morning interludes continue, and, as always, I use them for prayer, meditation, and exercise. I also devote some of that time to plotting new experiences. One vision Donte had was of us living in New York, leaving our penthouse, all of us dressed in black and going somewhere. Ever since he shared that with me, I knew it was something important to him, and it has stuck in my brain. Because I love him, his vision has become mine too. I'm committed to trying to create that experience. Whether we are at home in Nashville or New York or elsewhere, one thing I know. I will start the day at 4:30 with a prayer to God and the Universe. From there, the list of places, ideas, thoughts, and dreams my path will take me down is endless.

# CREATING YOUR OWN VISION BOARD

### EXERCISE EIGHT:
### *Sometimes Life Should Be About You*

What do you do or where do you go when you want space for yourself? How does that "me place" look? Is it a path in the woods? Maybe it's a library covered with books. Or a deck overlooking the park.

For the vision board you will be building, gather some images of the place or places where you regularly go to spend time by yourself. For me, one is the Belmont Park in Nashville where I take my early morning walks. Another is my home gym, complete with Peloton and weights.

For those who don't have such a retreat, take this as an opportunity to imagine one. No matter how busy you are, you should always have a place to escape and spend time by yourself on a regular basis. Nourishing yourself will give you the energy you need to help others.

# CHAPTER NINE

# BE ACCOUNTABLE

## THERE IS NO SUCH THING AS BAD LUCK

O n a recent Saturday afternoon, a paralegal whose firm was representing a client in a civil matter sent an urgent query to MediCopy. She had contacted us a couple of days earlier asking if we could help locate the client's medical records, and one of our team members had started the process. But now, with the deposition a couple of days away, she needed the files right away and reached out through the chat on the company's website. Could we expedite the process?

Our office was closed for the weekend. The customer service reps who handle the chat with clients are off Saturdays and Sundays, so the function is usually down. I was at home browsing the chat, caught the message, and responded. "Hey, I'm sorry, we don't open until

Monday. But let me see how I can help you." I was able to invoice, quality check, and email the documents to her in a matter of minutes.

For most business owners—especially heads of multimillion-dollar businesses—a scenario like that is unheard of. What owner is going to check the chat function on the company's website on a Saturday? And if by chance they do, most will leave it to a representative to handle when the business opens on Monday.

I—and MediCopy—work differently. I use the example—one of the hundreds like it in our records of client and customer experiences—to illustrate just how different we are.

Being accessible and responsive always is a routine part of how we operate. The company has more than four thousand physician offices, hospitals, and other clients. I give all of them my cell number and email and tell them to reach out if any problems come up. Whether they are a physician in Seattle, a hospital administrator in Texas, or a health clinic owner in Mississippi, they are my bosses. As such, they all have access to me—and other senior MediCopy team members. One reason we go to great ends to make ourselves available is that our competitors don't. Clients of most companies usually call an 800 number and talk to the switchboard operator to get patched into a customer service rep who may or may not know the answer. At MediCopy, I want them to have the option of going straight to the top to get immediate results.

**BEING ACCESSIBLE AND RESPONSIVE ALWAYS IS A ROUTINE PART OF HOW WE OPERATE.**

I consider urgency and availability to be a big part of accountability. And accountability is at the very heart of MediCopy's mission. It's our number one core value. I—and the entire team—have made it part of our culture and intrinsic in our daily operations.

# EARLY LESSONS IN TRUST

Like so many essential aspects of my life, my focus on being conscientious about answering questions and offering explanations is rooted in my childhood and adolescent experiences. My father frequently made promises to business clients that he knew he could not keep. During his extramarital affair and the divorce, he never sat me—or my mom—down and explained why he had opted to break the family apart. Since there was no accountability, trust was broken all the way around. I couldn't trust my father. Other family members weren't there for me after my father's passing, so I could not trust them either. It was hard for me to trust any outsiders.

Once I was out on my own, I witnessed other examples where the failure of accountability was glaring. One situation involved Allie and Jim, a couple I lived with when I was eighteen and between places to stay. One was a manager of a cookie store, and the other one assisted him. The store made $5,000 a day. They would take 10 percent of that—just swipe $500 from the register on top of their pay. They never questioned what they were doing, so it went on and on.

Jim was also working at a furniture company where one of the protocols was that if something was damaged you would just throw it away. He would mark items as broken and pretend to toss them in the dumpster. But he'd later go pick up the stuff and take it home.

On the one hand, they had an enviable lifestyle—drove great cars, constantly attended sports events, and enjoyed frequent vacations. On the other hand, they always fought. They were never happy. There was no remorse.

During that time, I slept on the sofa and mowed their grass so I could pay my way. I watched what they were doing with a mixture of intrigue and disbelief. Part of me was confused about how they could get away with this behavior. But the other part was thinking, "This is not right! What are y'all doing?"

With time, I decided to use the case studies of my father, of Allie and Jim—and similar situations I had seen—as teachable moments. I pledged to make trust front and center in my business—and my life.

During the infant years at MediCopy, I developed a good sense of the role accountability should play in a company. It started with ensuring that the lines of communication with our clients are always open. Of course, there was a lot more to it: going the extra mile in customer service, caring for all our team members, being straightforward about acknowledging when things go wrong. Perhaps most important, it meant being there to answer questions, mainly to explain why we did something. It's being able to accept ownership and say, "Yes, I did that. And this is why." Sometimes that's not as easy as it sounds. There are plenty of examples where someone may fully believe that whatever they did was the right thing to do even if others disagreed. After they explain the reasoning, it might make 100 percent sense.

# OUR CORE VALUES

MediCopy's culture of accountability extends beyond our dealing with clients to the way we manage our team. I make a point of interviewing every single person before they are hired. I go over our core values in those conversations, starting with my accountability commitment to team members. As they sit across from me, I tell every potential employee that I want them to continue to grow personally and professionally if they are hired. I assure them that they will get raises if they've met their quality standards, or KPIs, or other production goals. But they will also have my care and concern about their livelihoods.

If I have two hundred employees, I am worried about two hundred families, two hundred car notes, two hundred house payments, and two hundred or more schools. As new team members, they become part of that worry.

We carry through with the emphasis on accountability during the employee onboarding process. In a typical orientation event, we have freshly hired team members come into the office. Even though most will be working remotely, we want them to see the headquarters if they live close by. I give a presentation, telling them more about my background. I also explain that if they ever need anything personally or professionally, I am a chat away, and they should reach out. I always end by telling them that MediCopy is different from any other place they might have worked. I tell them that the baggage they carry from other workplaces—that manager who wouldn't listen, the director or CEO you never even met, or the ideas you came up with that you were too afraid to share with those people—should all be left outside our front door.

Once they start work, new team members start seeing that accountability at MediCopy is more than a slogan. In our weekly announcements, they read about a team member who's only been here a year but has worked their behind off and been promoted. Sometimes the reactions are reported back to me. "Oh, man," one team member was quoted as saying. "I do have a chance. When the boss said in the interview that every employee would move up, he wasn't just talking. These people are moving and shaking. They're making promotions around here."

I try to show my empathy for employees in personal ways too. Every year, at the end of the third and beginning of the fourth quarter, I email my entire team every other week, telling them how many checks are left in the year. I remind them to set a budget for Christmas and not overextend themselves and go into debt. I'm trying to help them because most bosses won't take the time to care. They don't care if their employees live paycheck to paycheck. I do. I see this as a small encouragement I can give to people to think outside the box.

In my efforts to help other team members, I often draw from my own life experiences. Not long ago, I had an employee who lost his father. He called me on the way to the funeral to talk to me about it. We were talking like friends. He was so upset with his family and needed to vent about how they were approaching the grieving process.

"You need to stop that," I told him. "You need to take control and do what your father would want you to do. Take it from me, somebody who's lost their dad; this is something that I pray and wish will happen to you."

"The most important thing for you to be worried about," I explained, "is how to give thanks for everything that he gave to you." All I was doing was transferring that energy of what I felt about my dad and what I would do and what I did with my father. And we kind of just had a moment together.

A day or two later, he sent me a six-minute-long voicemail summarizing the eulogy he gave at his dad's funeral. As I listened to it and heard that he had included a big part of what I had talked to him about, I could not help but be full of emotion.

# BEING LIABLE TO MYSELF AND MY FAMILY

My commitment to accountability extends beyond the business to my family and personal life. For starters, I make sure I am there for Isa, my daughter, providing her with everything she's ever needed or wanted. But I also teach her to be responsible and have accountability for the things that she's given, especially when it comes to the luxuries of life. She learned to wash clothes at five years old and to iron at seven, and she took the trash out every day.

I am liable to Donte as well. Fortunately, the business can afford a pretty good living for us. He has his sense of accountability and a game plan for himself and what he wants to do with his life. He has his mission as an artist. He converted one of the bedrooms into a studio so he can just go there to draw and do what he wants to do. That's his way of expressing his individuality and accountability to himself.

I also have the responsibility to be accountable to myself. I have work duties to fulfill. I also focus on personal growth, usually during the walks I take by myself in the mornings. I am aware that before I'm Isa's dad, I'm still Elliott. Before I'm Donte's husband, I'm Elliott first. We all take a similar perspective and respect that about each other.

> **I AM AWARE THAT BEFORE I'M ISA'S DAD, I'M STILL ELLIOTT. BEFORE I'M DONTE'S HUSBAND, I'M ELLIOTT FIRST.**

In our household, we all work independently and are accountable for our work and ourselves professionally. On a typical day, Donte and I work in our home office while our daughter is in her room doing her schoolwork.

We have set family times when, at various intervals during the day, we come together. We share lunch and dinner. And we talk about our day or what we need to do or our game plans or even decisions that need to be made as a family. We all know how precious those times are.

# STANDING BY OUR PRINCIPLES

Being true to our commitment to accountability has sometimes required MediCopy to cut its losses with clients. Fortunately, those instances have been rare. One such case involved a company we were working with in Ohio. They were very high maintenance, and we had four team members working on the account. Of the four thousand clients throughout the country that we work with, only a dozen or so are high maintenance. But this one asked for more attention than anyone else. They wanted weekly meetings. They insisted that their lawyers be in on every session. And they came to every meeting with complaints. It became a pattern. Each time we investigated their complaint, we found it was someone on their staff who was responsible. They gave us the issue, and then we had to examine it to find out it was them.

After months of this, I said, "Guys, we've got to get rid of them. This is a resource drainer. Yes, we're going to lose $250,000. But there's something else going on. It has nothing to do with us." We terminated that client.

The four MediCopy team members who worked the account were worried about their jobs. As it turned out, we got a new account within ten days, and they were assigned to manage it. In the end, the new account brought in double the revenue of the one we fired. And the team members were grateful that I had their backs, that I had faith in them, and that I wasn't going to put up with an unfairly difficult client because of the money. I showed that I valued people over profit, and they appreciated that.

Of course, there have been times when team members have had accountability issues. Fortunately, these cases have been rare. If an employee who has performed well in the past seems to hit a rough patch, I try to find out what's behind it. There was one such case not long ago of a team member who had been with me for seven years and had always been cheerful and optimistic. But they got into a terrible space, both personally and professionally. My initial response was to take them to lunch and figure out what we could do to change the course. They had given up on themselves, and it's hard to invest in someone when they've reached that stage. I just told them, "This is not a good fit any longer. It's okay that I'm a stepping-stone for you."

For every client we have had to let go or a team member who hasn't worked out, dozens have benefited from our commitment to accountability. Not long ago, a team member in Kentucky wrote to report that she'd just purchased her first home. "Without someone like you, who is encouraging, motivating, inspirational, I'm not sure if I would be able to do this, or pull the trigger to do it," she told me.

Our clients and customers also send in regular expressions of gratitude. Hundreds of them have reviewed us on Google, and an overwhelming majority have awarded us the top five-star rating. "MediCopy representatives are some of the nicest people I've ever worked with," one reviewer said.

Working with us felt "like holding my hands, the first time walking across the street," said another. The paralegal from California who we worked with to expedite a request also wrote in a review. "I wish every company was like MediCopy," she said.

It's feedback like this that makes going the extra mile worthwhile.

# CREATING YOUR OWN VISION BOARD

### EXERCISE NINE:
### Composing Your Accountability Chart

Start by making two lists. The first should be composed of all of the people in your life to whom you are accountable. The second should be of all of the people who you consider accountable to you. (In many cases, the lists will overlap.)

One idea for your vision board is to start with a picture of you at the center. Surrounding you in an inner circle will be all of those on the first list. In the outer circle place those on the second list. Give each person a caption specifying the way accountability works in any relationship.

Include that circle in the vision board you will make when you finish the book.

## CHAPTER TEN

# EVERYONE HAS A VISION

## TEAM MEMBERS SHARE THEIR DREAMS

Inspiring MediCopy's team members—and my close family and friends—to have dreams and pursue them is a big part of my approach to being an active boss. Over the course of hiring, training, and managing hundreds of people, I have found that getting people who have never dreamed much to start dreaming can be a hard sell. Most folks are too preoccupied with paying mortgages, school fees, and other bills to look beyond the week, let alone make plans for next year.

Vision boards are good, tangible tools to get people fired up for the process of thinking about their future. In previous chapters, I have discussed how they have helped me focus and center my aspirations in MediCopy and other aspects of my life. This is why I encourage the entire staff to make their own boards. As I noted in chapter 8, I give every team member time off to make their board, and I offer prizes to the most compelling boards.

Even with those incentives, many new team members are still reluctant about the boards. One example is Damon Reid. In his first year as a sales manager, Damon skipped my push for everyone to make one. "I didn't understand what they were about," he said. "So, I took a pass." Blake McConnell, who came on thirteen years ago as an account manager, had a similar reaction. Ashley Ayers, an artist at heart, was intrigued about the boards when I started pitching the idea. But she was unsure how to create one. Even Donte, my husband, who joined the MediCopy staff in 2015, did not focus on the concept of vision boards until the buzz about them started in the office.

And yet, once each of them focused on the boards, they got deeply engaged in the process. Each of their journeys with the boards—and their broader paths creating life plans—is different and compelling. I thought it best that they share the experiences they have had in their own words. Their narratives reflect the experiences that many MediCopy team members end up embracing and building their visions.

## DAMON REID, SALES MANAGER

Before I joined MediCopy in 2017, I had never heard of a vision board. I had started working part time, only Thursdays and Fridays. I didn't know much about the company's culture or values. Elliott sent out a vision board memo, encouraging everyone to join the process, but I brushed it off. I opted not to participate at all.

Then Elliott called me into his office. "You've been here for six months," he said. "It is imperative that you do a vision board. The due date has passed, and you can't win anything. But you need to throw something together because I want to see it." At that moment, I felt like I was in trouble for not doing an art project. Naturally, out of respect for the request from the boss, I fulfilled it. But that first board was rudimentary, only pictures glued to a piece of paper. It was not my proudest moment.

In response, Elliott summoned me once again. He showed me his vision board and broke it down, picture by picture, vision by vision. His presentation resonated with me. It was the first time anyone—from my very accomplished family or any other corner of my life—had ever sat me down and looked me in the eyes and told me they care about where I want to be and they want to help me get there. For once, someone gave me the time and energy to say they wanted me to focus on myself and that they would be there to help me in any way they could.

*FOR ONCE, SOMEONE GAVE ME THE TIME AND ENERGY TO SAY THEY WANTED ME TO FOCUS ON MYSELF.*

The following year—2018—I put a lot of work and thought into my board. And to my surprise, I won the competition. More importantly, the visions I put on that board began to come to fruition. I had put the word *promotion* up there, for example. And I got one. I like to travel. I'd never been to Chicago. Nor had I traveled abroad. I was curious to see those destinations. So I put trips to Chicago and Mexico on the board too. In that year, I visited both and loved them. Besides helping me discover the world, it helped me follow through on the need for a work/life balance—something I learned at MediCopy.

Once I saw the positive powers the board could bring, I began putting work into it. Part of that meant being more ambitious in my visions. I had been thinking of moving to Chicago, so I put that on the board. I had dreams of continuing my education. So, I put both of those on the board. If all goes according to plan, next year I will relocate to Chicago and start school. I will continue my work at MediCopy but in a different role.

Looking back, it's clear to me why Elliott pushed me to create a vision board. The boards have helped me focus on my future.

# ASHLEY AYERS, COMPLIANCE

When I first came to MediCopy, the staff was small—only around thirty people, compared with more than seven times that number now. Elliott would go from one employee to the next, preaching the importance of life planning. "You need to set goals for yourself," he would say. "Where do you want to be in five years?"

I remember when he came to me, I was sweaty and nervous.

I was in my early twenties and living day by day. My job at that time was front-desk receptionist. I didn't have any plans. I wasn't thinking about what to do to better myself. I was not posing the kind of questions that Elliott liked—such as what type of energy I wanted to put out into the world or what kind of energy I wanted to take in. I wasn't looking five years ahead. My drifting was likely at least partly because I had experienced significant trauma earlier in my life and did not have a close relationship with my family.

"You should start doing some planning," he said. "It could be something small such as 'I want to save five dollars a week.' Or 'I want to start taking a walk every morning.'"

He started challenging me to do those things. Then he introduced vision boards.

On my early boards, I included yoga, cooking, and gardening. In that period, I was trying to understand the trauma I had been through. I wanted to navigate my world better. To do that, I felt as if I needed to figure out healthier tools to be a better person and a better worker and to further my career. I followed through and started doing yoga, gardening, and some cooking.

On my 2017 board, I put therapy. Donald Trump had been elected, and it shook me. I knew I needed help to deal with it. I went on to start therapy sessions that year.

In 2019, I narrowed my goals and focused on them. I concentrated on specific things that I wanted to get accomplished that year. One was buying a new mattress. Another was saving money. And a third was to improve my credit score. I eventually wanted to buy a new car. But instead of putting up a picture of a car, I mapped out the things I needed to do to get there. Over that year, I knocked out everything on that board: I improved my credit score, saved money, and bought a mattress. And the following year, I bought a new car.

Professional goals are also something that has become a regular feature of my vision boards. I have added promotions to my boards. And I have consistently obtained them. From my initial front-desk job, I have moved up step by step. I am now a manager in the compliance department.

More recently, I have taken life planning a step further than the vision boards.

I talked to my partner about vision boards and showed the types of things I was doing to map out how to fulfill my plans. I bought him a variety of planners called a "Passion Road Map." I sat down with him and showed him my passion road map. He picked up on it.

Now he makes his vision boards. He also buys one of these planners every year and completes them. And they're kind of like our ideas, like a joint vision board.

This all started years ago with Elliott telling me I had to have goals.

# BLAKE McCONNELL,
## DIRECTOR OF OPERATIONS

My story is an excellent example of how realizing your visions can be a long-term effort.

When Elliott first started talking about vision boards, I thought I had heard of them before, but I didn't really put much thought into it.

In my first year at MediCopy, I did not participate in making boards. But then I became familiar with Elliott's story. The way he imagined or had a vision for this company and then created it impressed me. It inspired me to start making my vision boards.

On my first effort creating a board, I put owning a home. I also included meeting someone special and getting married. Another vision I had was going to New York and seeing Broadway plays. And another was seeing Dolly Parton. I know that's a little cliché, but she always touched me growing up. Going to one of her concerts would be like going to heaven for me. I had professional ambitions too, and made them a part of my early boards. I put becoming chief operating officer at MediCopy on one. At the time, I was an intro-level account manager, a job I got by responding to an ad on Craigslist.

A couple of years after I highlighted owning a home on my board, I started looking at houses. It took a while, but I eventually found one I loved and started the process of buying it.

At the time I put getting married on my board, I was on the dating scene. I started having a conversation with Elliott about finding the right match. He shared with me that finding someone with your values can take time. But he reassured me that it would happen. And then, a couple of years later—five years ago—I met Eric. We started dating, and things became increasingly serious. Three years after that, we got married. It was a small ceremony. Elliott was my best man.

Something similar happened with my job. I gradually worked my way up from account manager, getting a promotion every year. And now I am director of operations. I work side by side with Elliott, kind of as a right-hand man. Among other things, I interview people for the same job I had when I started.

**ONE BIG MORAL IN ALL THIS IS THAT IT CAN TAKE A WHILE FOR VISIONS TO COME TRUE.**

Nine years after putting my hope of seeing Dolly Parton on my vision board, it had not happened. Tickets are pretty expensive, and I hadn't snagged one. And then, unexpectedly, last year, Elliott gifted two tickets to one of her concerts for my husband and me for my birthday. They were front row seats at the Grand Ole Opry.

For me, one big moral in all this is that it can take a while for visions to come true. But if you focus and work on them, thoughts do indeed become things.

# DONTE NOBLE-HOLT

Initially, I didn't focus much on the boards, mostly because I was transitioning from Jersey to Nashville. Once the move was complete, I started working at MediCopy, and everyone was talking vision boards.

I made one. I put on it the things that came to my mind, primarily random ideas.

Gradually my approach to them has evolved. In preparation for making one, I think, "Okay, what do I want this board to say? What do I want this year? What's something that maybe happened this year, but I want to build upon? What didn't happen this year, but I would like to happen the following year?" Or just something that I'm looking forward to, and I want it to be excellent.

On my board in 2019, I put on there something about the performing artist Kylie Minogue. And I put London as a destination I would like to visit. Then, that year we ended up going on a vacation to London. And there we saw Minogue in concert. It turned out to be a perfect trip and a fabulous show.

And then, on that same board, I put a photo of Janet Jackson. We had just seen her in concert. "I don't know why I'm putting her here again," I said to myself. "But I feel like there's something that's going to happen." Sure enough, we saw her again in concert the following year. After the show, we met her at a backstage meet-and-greet. *Wow,* I thought. *That was something I never expected to happen.*

Of course, not every vision becomes a reality. One year I put shoes on the board. It was supposed to represent us starting a retail shoe store. But then, the pandemic came, and the store never happened. It's a good thing it didn't because we would very likely have lost a lot of money.

One constant that has been on my board for some years is having kids with Elliott. It's probably the most significant thing on my board for 2021. Very exciting. I put it up on my early boards as just a thought. Then Elliott and I started talking about it.

Now it's back on my board. As we go through the surrogacy process, I see it's happening. It's a big vision coming true.

## CHAPTER ELEVEN

# EVOLVING THE VISION

## MAKING ADJUSTMENTS AS YOU MOVE FORWARD

**N**ot long ago, as I watched a football game, I became absorbed with the way one of the teams maneuvered. I will call them Team A. They burst out on the field with a strong start, had a well-developed game plan, and moved into the lead. Team B came back with an impressive defense, requiring Team A to alter its strategy. As the game proceeded, some opportunities emerged out of nowhere. At one point, for instance, a top Team A receiver found himself way downfield and wide open. They deftly took advantage of that, giving them a touchdown. And there were other such moments. In the end, they won the game pretty handily.

Afterward, I realized why Team A had grabbed my attention: they reminded me a lot of MediCopy. As the team coach at my business, I started with a solid vision, just as I imagined the Team A coach had. In my case, it was to build a medical records business with superior customer service. During more than two decades of operations, some significant changes happened—in the medical services industry, in the company, and in my journey as a business owner and boss. Each new or unexpected turn in the road called on me to make adjustments in the way I ran the company—and managed my life. I devote this chapter to discussing the most significant changes and how I have dealt with them.

The first unexpected boon at MediCopy was early runaway success. Earlier in the book, I talked about the day during our first year when I realized that I could make over $1,000, working only half a day. By my calculations, that meant I could take home $10,000 a week and half a million dollars a year. I just had to hustle to get clients to make that happen. Soon after that, the company started reaching more significant and impressive milestones. It was clear that if we made the right moves, we could have far greater revenues than $1,000 a day. Eventually we hit a million in revenues, and I continued to set higher goals: $2 million, $3 million, $4 million, $10 million, and eventually $30 million. I also wanted my team to have the same success both personally and professionally that I had. Doing this without outside investors and capital and remaining debt-free was a considerable accomplishment.

Of course, early success is a problem every start-up would love to have. The challenge was how to keep up that record as the company grew, how to deliver the same high level of personal, efficient customer experience to over four thousand clients that we gave to our first fifty clients. It's all about scaling up and maintaining authenticity— something that is common among many new companies.

For us, making the right moves came down to four things:

Hiring the right people. This is one reason why I am personally committed to interviewing all new employees.

Training the team in what is expected of them and compensating them appropriately.

Constantly communicating with clients. This has meant keeping the lines of contact open for questions, comments, or criticism.

Making sure that every action we took aligned with our core values. This has meant asking questions such as: "Are we being open and honest by letting a salaried employee leave two hours early every Friday while others are there to pick up that person's slack?" Or "Are we helping people's personal and professional growth, even if it means them leaving the business or helping them with their education?" When we achieved 100 percent alignment in the company's leadership, it trickled down to other team members.

Following these basic steps has earned us twenty-one consecutive years of growth. In 2021, MediCopy was valued at between $70 and $100 million.

Another significant change came when medical records became digital. The Health Information Technology for Economic and Clinical Health Act of 2009, introduced by then-President Obama, pumped $27 billion of federal incentives into adopting electronic health records (EHR) and electronic medical records (EMR) in the US. That forced doctors to adapt quickly to often complex EMR/EHR systems. Most physicians were ill-prepared to deal with the changes and became frustrated. MediCopy was able to position itself to assist doctors across the US. We devised strategies to go remotely into physicians' offices and hospitals' new medical records systems. These steps gave us a much broader national reach. They also allowed us to partner with healthcare professionals throughout the US.

We expanded to the Cloud, something that back then was new to everyone. We partnered with Box.com, which allowed us to store millions of patients' records securely and share them as needed. We began to hire employees all across the country. This created the path for us to bring our Tennessee charm and core values to patients, attorneys, and insurance companies nationwide.

Digitization, in turn, helped transform MediCopy from a regional to a national business with far more clients and team members. It was clear that we needed a more sophisticated way of managing operations. I felt that I could benefit from the insights of more experienced business owners and so turned to a handful of trusted outside advisors for suggestions on how to guide the company forward. One was Scott Hallman, a consultant. He had owned a medical records business in the 1980s and had sold it to my most significant competitor. We would have a monthly conference call, and he was able to give me some important lessons. The biggest and most important takeaway from those meetings was about the power of optimization. What that meant was learning to charge for all of our services. If we were fielding one hundred medical records requests a day, for example, and we wanted to make this amount of money, we had to know what to charge for that. If we were able to bill a certain amount for affidavits, UPS fees, or other expenses, charge that. After a couple of years, I had grasped the concept and run with it.

I also joined the Entrepreneurs Organization, or EO, the group of business owners I mentioned earlier in the book. I attended regular meetings online and worked closely with a couple of local members.

The success in marketing and sales at MediCopy had led us to keep beefing up the staff. And yet, we had no fundamental management structure. We had no HR, no training, no compliance. There was nobody in charge of change management or operations. We had one person in IT. Otherwise, it was me interacting directly with the team. I was a bald, bearded boss, but the system was not efficient.

My colleagues in EO tutored me in developing and training managers. They drew from the experiences they had in bringing in new division heads. I leaned heavily on two of the members of the group who were based in Nashville. One was Bob, who owned a group of local restaurants. The other, Michael, was in the software business. His company sold to different hospital systems. They were in

**MY COLLEAGUES IN EO TUTORED ME IN DEVELOPING AND TRAINING MANAGERS.**

growth mode both personally and professionally. I was attracted to their focus on scaling up and to their can-do forward-leaning spirit. We met regularly at one of Bob's restaurants and talked about business growth and all it entails. I was so motivated and inspired that I wanted to learn what they knew to have something similar in my business.

My close engagement with the EO and with Bob and Michael started in 2012. When we fast-forward a decade, lots of things had changed. Michael had long since sold his business. MediCopy was bringing in more revenue and had more value than Michael's company had when he transitioned out of it. MediCopy had developed a strong leadership team with eight people on it. We had a director of operations, a director of change management, a client engagement team, a sales team, a director of compliance, and a whole compliance team. This team of managers makes a colossal difference. I don't have to worry about those things. I could keep my eyes on the culture and the refinement of the vision.

# DOING BUSINESS IN THE PANDEMIC

COVID-19 was another dilemma that required making adjustments. Throughout the pandemic of 2020–21, MediCopy performed well as a business. I worked remotely, and so did almost all two hundred of our employees. Regretfully, one team member lost her mother to COVID-19, but otherwise the personal fallout was kept to a minimum. Our calls were answered in a timely fashion. Our production quality went up. Business kept coming in, and we kept handling it. There were occasions when we had so much work that I offered double-time to those who wanted to work Friday, Saturday, and Sunday.

In April 2021, I conducted a survey of those working at home, asking if they would prefer to keep working remotely, come into the office, or do a hybrid model. I made it clear that for me, their safety is the most important thing. But I also told them that maintaining the company culture and keeping performance goals were also key. Ninety-nine percent said they would opt to stay at home. When asked to cite a reason, most said that working remotely allowed them to spend more time with family and for themselves.

I decided to allow any employee who was tenured pre-COVID to stay at home as long as their productivity and quality remained at the same level or higher than when they were in the office. For the foreseeable future, around two hundred of our team members will be remote.

New employees will come into the office and receive training there.

Working from the office will be good for them because it will allow them to become familiar with the company culture. Once they start meeting their goals in 90 to 120 days, they will have the chance to work remotely.

In the end, the pandemic has shown us that we can do just as well if not better work without the hassle of commutes, out-of-town business trips, trade shows, and in-person conferences.

As MediCopy matured, and I became more adept at my role as chief strategist and keeper of the culture, I have had an Awakening. With age I get the feeling that I'm about to enter a different life and lifestyle. I don't know if the process will involve transitioning away from the business or if God and the Universe are pushing me to do even more in some other form. But what I sense happening is a mission to spread the gospel of what I have learned and experienced to broader audiences.

I don't think that God wants to use me only through the medium of MediCopy to affect its two hundred team members. I believe He wants to use me to reach as many people as possible, including those I know and others I don't yet know. It's a calling, not unlike those that preachers have. I don't see myself in a church. But I want to talk about God and the Universe's impact on my life and what it can do for other people. I want to show them that if they just stopped, centered themselves, focused, came up with an action plan, and then executed it, they could live the way they wanted. So many people are stuck in a rut and can't move from it. They don't know which way to turn.

*I WANT TO TALK ABOUT GOD AND THE UNIVERSE'S IMPACT ON MY LIFE AND WHAT IT CAN DO FOR OTHER PEOPLE.*

I see myself in a position to guide them. I have already begun to answer that call with *Bald Bearded Boss*, including a podcast and this book. Together these media speak to who I am and touch on how I overcame obstacles and life experiences from divorce, death, and losing my inheritance to become a successful father, son, husband, and entrepreneur.

My next book, *The Formula*, will lay the groundwork for readers to navigate life experiences using the same approaches I have employed. I will explore all the various issues I have faced. That list is long: overcoming childhood trauma, being different, divorce, grief, finding the right one, being a parent, taking care of a parent, starting a business, and preparing for new stages or phases of your life.

*The Formula* will explain how to find a path forward from each of these challenges. It will detail how to use the tools I used—practical and spiritual practices, habits, consistency, action, power of manifestation, open and honest communication with others and yourself—and how to create a list of core values to live by.

I hope that joining me on the journey to becoming a Bald Bearded Boss has been helpful. Please stay tuned for the next phase.

# CREATING YOUR OWN VISION BOARD

## EXERCISE TEN:
### Sharing the Vision Board Experience

For this exercise, invite four or five people in your inner circle to make their own vision boards. The group could be work colleagues, your significant other, close friends, or family. Since the concept may be new to many of them, I recommend hosting a meetup or vision board gathering where you walk them through the thinking behind vision boards. You can even make it a party in which you bring poster boards, glue, magazines, and photographs and kick everyone off making their own boards.

Make it an annual event, so that each of you can discuss how you put action behind your vision and manifested it. Be sure to celebrate your success!

# ACKNOWLEDGMENTS

Dad, thank you for the work ethic you instilled in me and for showing me what it means to be a provider. Thank you for watching over me all these years. I hope I have made you proud!

Mom, thank you for showing me how to love, be compassionate, forgive, and give back. I will continue to honor you and dad. I miss you!

Isa, my unconditional love for you has challenged me to be the best father I could be without any real guidance. I hope you forgive me for any shortcomings. I will love you forever.

Donte, without you, I would have less laughter, smiles, and *Real Housewives* to watch. You truly balance me out and I am thankful to God and the Universe for bringing me and you together. I love you!